LIFE ACCORDING TO
FREDDIE FLINTOFF

LIFE ACCORDING TO
FREDDIE FLINTOFF

DO YOU KNOW WHAT?

BLINK

bringing you closer

Published by Blink Publishing
2.25, The Plaza,
535 Kings Road,
Chelsea Harbour,
London, SW10 0SZ

www.blinkpublishing.co.uk

facebook.com/blinkpublishing
twitter.com/blinkpublishing

Hardback – 978-1-788-700-46-7
Ebook – 978-1-788-700-45-0

A CIP catalogue of this book is available from the British Library.

Typeset by seagulls.net
Printed and bound in Great Britain by Clays Ltd, Elcograf S.p.A.

5 7 9 10 8 6 4

Blink Publishing is an imprint of Bonnier Books UK
www.bonnierbooks.co.uk

CONTENTS

PROLOGUE

Earlier this year, I found myself treading the boards in musical theatre. Not for the first time in my life, I thought to myself, 'How did I get here?' But it was definitely me, singing on a stage. Not particularly well, but doing it anyway.

This is a book about the unpredictability of life, with all its glory and disappointments. It is a book about having a go, even when the odds are stacked against you. It is a book about not giving a shit what anybody else thinks. There are incredible things to experience beyond your comfort zone.

There is a bit of cricket, because it's the game that made me and the game I still love. There are my thoughts on celebrity and what it means to be a working-class bloke from Preston with a stylist, a make-up man and a Lamborghini that never gets driven. There is romance and there are pranks and the mistakes of youth. There are things that get my goat and the strange things that amaze me. There is even a little bit of politics.

There are also some things that are particularly close to my heart, because life hasn't always been easy. I drank too much and have struggled with eating disorders and mental illness.

I hope that by sharing my experiences, I might be able to help people. And there is, of course, my wonderful family.

I would hesitate to call this a book of lessons, because I'm not the sort of bloke who shouts the odds through a megaphone. I'm not entirely sure men have been to the moon or whether the Earth is flat, and I sometimes wonder what does and doesn't matter in life and whether any of this actually exists. But I hope we have a rapport, and that you see where I'm coming from. It's not easy sometimes, because I struggle to make sense of where I've been, but I hope you enjoy the ride as much as me.

CHAPTER 1

IN (ALMOST) TOO DEEP

Life beyond the comfort zone

I'm standing in a wrestling ring in a warehouse in Florida, surrounded by dozens of cameras, filming me from every conceivable angle. What looks like the entire cast of *Game of Thrones* are ringside, all wearing fluorescent Lycra. And all I can think is: 'I just want to get out of here.'

Before I know it, someone has shoved a microphone in my hand and shouted in my ear, 'Right, now your turn.' No going back now. Two minutes doesn't sound like much, but when you're so far out of your comfort zone you need satnav to find your way back, it feels like an eternity.

I launch into my routine, which I thought up during the walk to the ring: 'I'm from Preston, England, and I'm gonna hammer all of you and shake things up!'

It still makes me cringe just thinking about it. But as I'm climbing out of the ring, I think to myself, 'That was rubbish. I want another crack at it.'

I snatch the microphone back, climb back in and take in my surroundings for a few seconds. Everywhere I look there are weird and wonderful people, and I pick out a few obvious targets – a fella with a massive head, a fella with a big nose, a fella with a particularly bad haircut, a fella with a stupid voice – and let rip. The fella with a head like a melon gets it good and proper, big nose doesn't know what's hit him, the bloke with the man-bun looks like he might start crying. Two minutes go by and I can see the director trying to wind me up out of the corner of my eye, but I start shouting at him like a maniac, 'Oh no, I have not finished yet, just you try and stop me...' I'm like a man possessed. At this rate, wind-up man is going to have to wrench the microphone from my cold, dead hands.

My routine lasts ten minutes, and as I'm climbing out of the ring for the second time, all I can hear is absolute silence. Everyone else got a clap. I sit back down, feeling a bit self-conscious, and watch the room empty.

The acting coach comes over and says, 'That was good, well done.'

'Thanks, mate, but I don't think the others liked it much.'

'Don't worry about them. You can teach anyone to wrestle, but you've got to be able to get a reaction from the audience, whether good or bad. Wrestling fans hate vanilla. And one thing you weren't was vanilla.'

How did I end up in a wrestling ring in Tampa? It's a fair question – wrestling isn't a typical career progression for a former England cricketer. The simple answer is, I needed a job. I was living in Dubai at the time, drinking too much, eating anything I wanted, cruising through life. My day consisted of taking the kids to school at 7:30 – I'm not an early riser, so that was a nightmare, especially after a heavy night – before heading to the gym at the Burj Al Arab. The Burj is a six-star hotel, and ridiculous for it, because you don't have to do anything. You park your car and someone appears out of nowhere to take your keys. Someone carries your bag to the gym. You meet your bag at the gym and as you're getting undressed, a man is picking your clothes up to wash them. You get in the gym and as you're trying to put weights on the bar, someone steps in to do it for you. I'm surprised they don't offer to run for you as well.

After the gym, I'd sit on the beach for two or three hours. Every day I'd eat a fruit platter, because it was the cheapest thing on the menu, but it still cost about 30 quid. Then I'd go out and drink aimlessly in the evenings, and if I'd carried on like that I would have been skint. As it was, I was in a restaurant one night and both of my credit cards bounced. I looked around in a panic and saw the football manager Steve Bruce on another table. We had a mutual friend, so I went over and said, 'All right, Steve, nice to meet you. I'm a big fan, so and so says hello.' Then, after a while, I said, 'Look, Steve, bit of a problem, I can't pay my bill. Can you lend us a few quid?' That was my life in Dubai, but it wasn't really living.

In television, everyone is looking for a hook. So you've got to put yourself out there and throw ideas at people, and if it all starts sounding like that scene from *Alan Partridge*, when he's desperately pitching programme ideas to Tony Hayers, the fictional BBC commissioning editor – 'Arm-wrestling with Chas and Dave? Inner-city Sumo? Monkey tennis?' – that's all right, because someone will bite eventually if they think your idea has legs.

While I was sat on the beach, contemplating the fact that the grape I was eating probably cost £5 on its own, I thought about all the things that interested me, and settled on wrestling. When I was a kid, I'd watch WWE – WrestleMania, Royal Rumble – and even Big Daddy and Giant Haystacks of a Saturday afternoon on ITV. So I thought, 'Why not have a go?'

My original idea was to get trained up and fight The Undertaker at the Manchester Arena. I pitched my idea to my then management team, they thought it might work, we wrote up a treatment, presented it to Sky, and they loved it. Sky put me in touch with Vince McMahon, the boss of WWE, he gave it the thumbs-up and invited me over to train at the WWE's performance centre in Tampa, where American wrestling wannabes try out for a place in the big time. All of a sudden it was no longer a daydream: this mad idea I came up with on a beach in Dubai was actually going to happen.

To say I was a bit out of shape is an understatement. If I'm being completely honest, I'd completely let myself go. So I flew a trainer over to Dubai for six weeks (not a sentence I ever thought I'd write when I was a kid growing up on a council estate in Preston), got myself fit and bulked myself up, so that I thought I was massive. But no sooner had me and the missus arrived in Tampa, I thought that maybe this wasn't the place for us. We were sat there waiting for our bags to come off, next to this big American fella, and he let out this almighty fart. I said to the missus, 'Did you hear that?'

She replied, 'Yes, I did.'

He did it again, so I said to him, 'Mate, are you all right there?' and he looked at me like I was daft, as if lifting your leg and letting rip in the middle of an airport was the most natural thing in the world. Not for the first time on that trip, I thought to myself, 'These might not be my kind of people...'

The next morning, a car picks me up to take me to the wrestling school, and the missus decides she wants to come with me. We arrive at this unit, open the car door and this fella walks past who looks like he's come straight from the cantina in *Star Wars*. He's about six foot eight inches and 300 pounds of pure muscle, with a head on him the size of a basketball. This isn't a case of wondering if he's my kind of person, this is a case of wondering if he's a person at all.

My missus says to me, 'Are you sure you're all right with this?'

I reply, 'I'm fine, I'm fine.'

I'm not fine at all, I am absolutely shitting myself.

I walk in the gym and there are all these gigantic blokes staring at me, at which point I say to the missus, 'Go back to the hotel, I've got this.' Which is code for, 'I haven't got this at all, but you really don't need to see what's about to happen.' So off she goes, leaving me with about 60 of the biggest, frostiest men in the world, all of them thinking, 'Who does this lad think he is? This is my dream, and this lad thinks he can just pop in and steal it from me...'

We start off with a warm-up, and the only person speaking to me is this massive lad from Wales, who knows me from the cricket, and is probably thinking, 'Where did it all go wrong?', but is too polite to say anything. Once we've warmed up, everyone stands around the ring to watch people chuck each other about, and after about five minutes they put me in there.

I'm standing there in my shorts in the middle of the ring, this other fella gets in with me, and I have to 'run the ropes', which is when you leg it across the ring, bounce off the ropes, barge into your opponent, and he picks you up and throws you on the canvas. After being thrown a few times, I think I'm going to swap with someone else. But it turns out I don't swap, the person who's throwing me does. For two hours, I'm bouncing off the ropes and getting thrown on the canvas. I did a bit of gymnastics as a kid, so could do a few flips, but nobody has taught me how to do this, so it's a case of suck it and see.

After a ten-minute break and a drink of water, I'm back in the ring, only this time I've got these monsters running at me, and I'm throwing them on the canvas. But every time I throw one of them, they front up to me, as if they want to do me in, because I'm not supposed to be picking them up and ramming them into the floor, I'm supposed to be lowering them down, almost as if we're dancing. Nobody has bothered telling me this either, so everybody hates me even more than when I first walked in.

After lunch, people are leapfrogging over me, and I'm leap-frogging over them, and I get so tired that when this one fella jumps over me, I can't get back up, and I stagger across the ring like I'm pissed and fall straight through the ropes. As I'm falling, I hook my leg on the top rope, face-plant the apron and bust my nose, so there's blood everywhere. Meanwhile, the missus is sat by the pool drinking her fourth piña colada of the day.

That evening, I get out of the shower and the missus looks at my body in complete shock. I'm bruised all over and can barely put my clothes on. We go and have some dinner and a few drinks to loosen up a bit, and then it all starts again the next morning. By lunchtime, it's starting to wear a bit thin, and when this fella starts taking the piss out of me, doing these stupid impressions, I'm thinking, 'I'm gonna have to put a stop to this, otherwise the next two weeks are going to be hell on earth.'

So I jump in the ring and say to him, 'Mate, I'd stop that right now.'

'Or what?'

'You're going to have to put all those muscles of yours on your chin, because that's where I'm going to belt you.'

As soon as I say it I think, 'Oh my God, what have I done? If he goes off, I've got nothing. I've brought a butter knife to a gun fight...' Luckily, he backs down, and I get accepted a little bit more by the rest of them.

That afternoon, I start getting a really bad pain in my side, to the point where I can't go any further. I say, 'Look, I think I'm having a back spasm', and the whole room goes up laughing – 'Hey, look at this goddamn Limey!' Oh, great. I take myself off to the physio room and as the bloke is manipulating my back, I can feel my ribs separating and I'm in agony.

I say, 'Mate, I think I've broken my ribs.'

'You've not broken your ribs, you'd be in too much pain.'

'Mate, I want to cry.'

He's still laughing when he sends me off for an X-ray, telling everyone within earshot, 'This guy thinks he's got broken ribs! What an idiot!'

In the specialist's room, there are pictures everywhere of all the famous wrestlers – The Undertaker, Hulk Hogan, 'Stone Cold' Steve Austin, even Kendo Nagasaki is probably up on his wall somewhere. There are also capes, masks, Lycra outfits, so that it's more like a wrestling museum than a surgery. He gets this X-ray out, sticks it on that machine they stick X-rays on, points to these two broken ribs and says, 'You've got two broken ribs.'

I say, 'I know.'

He asks me what I do and I tell him I'm a wrestler. He asks me how long I've been doing it and I tell him a day and a half. He says, 'Do you think it's for you?'

I reply, 'I don't think it is, to be honest with you...'

When I return to the gym, I'm waving my X-rays around like Neville Chamberlain just back from his meeting with Hitler – 'Peace in our time!' Soon word gets around that I've been wrestling with two broken ribs and suddenly people think I'm an all right bloke. The problem being, I've still got ten days to go.

Next day, I turn up at the gym knowing I can't do anything physical, but when I look around the gym, everyone is practising these pieces to camera, literally roaring about an inch away from the lens, covering it in phlegm. About 20 minutes later, I'm up in the ring with a microphone in my hand, shouting at the fella with a head like a melon, big nose and man-bun, telling them I'm going to take them all to the cleaners. Sometimes, when you think you're in too deep and might be drowning, you've just got to shut your eyes and swing. More of that in a bit.

Because I can't do any of the physical stuff, I say to the missus, 'We're here now, why don't we just go to Miami?' So the missus finds a place and we head down there.

We walk into this lovely art deco hotel called the Delano and the fella says, 'This is reception, but in the evening it turns into a nightclub. And I've got to warn you, it's the sort of place where men will try to hit on your woman.'

'If that happens, that's not gonna end well.'

'Well, if your woman doesn't show any interest, they might try and hit on you.'

I'm standing there thinking, 'This is gonna end very badly.'

'Do you want me to show you to your room?'

'No, I've got this, I've stayed in hotels before, just show me where the lift is and I'll find it myself.'

'Let me show you up anyway, so I can explain the room to you...'

We're in this hotel room, which is very nice, and this fella is pointing out all the obvious things, like the mini-bar and the safe, and just as I'm about to ask him if there's a kettle and some shortbread, he opens up this big box and starts pulling things out. I'm standing there with the missus thinking, 'What the hell is he up to?' And then it dawns on me: it's a sex-toy war chest.

I'm from Preston, where ribbed condoms are the height of sexual experimentation, so I haven't always been so open-minded. But here's this fella showing us all these dildos and vibrators and lots of other things whose correct usage I couldn't even guess at, some of them in shapes I didn't even know existed. There are handcuffs, blindfolds and rings for just about everything. If Willy Wonka did sex hotels, this place would be it. I thought it was a normal hotel, but the missus obviously got a good deal on Teletext.

For the next ten days, I lie by the pool and do not move. There are celebrities and footballers roaming all over the place, and as each day goes on, the pool turns into a nightclub. There's all sorts going on, so that it gets to the point where I think, 'I'm not swimming in that.' I drink rosé from 10am until I go to bed, undo all the training I've done, so that when I finally prise myself away from the sunbed and catch the plane home, I'm fatter than I was before.

I think nothing more of it for a while, just chalk it up as getting beaten up for two days with a free holiday in a high-class porn dungeon tagged on the end. But a few weeks later, I receive a message from someone at WWE, saying they've seen my piece to camera, seen me wrestle, and really like me. I can't do my documentary because I'll give all their secrets away, but they do want me to 'join them'. I tell them I don't understand what they mean — join them for what? — and they say they want me to come to wrestling school, and that they'd like to fast-track me in 18 months. They're promising me Wrestle-Mania, Royal Rumble, millions of dollars, the lot. I've never seen money like it.

Problem is, we're in Dubai, and planning to move home because we really want the kids to grow up in England. And I'm bored of sitting on the beach all day eating £5 grapes. I've got no friends and no life, but I don't want to up sticks and move to Tampa, where people drop their guts, right out in the open, and think it's normal. And because they pay their wrestlers so much, WWE essentially own you, you're at their beck and call, and it's me who'd be running about in my underpants in front of millions of people.

I politely decline, but they leave the door open. Apparently, wrestlers are in their prime between 35 and 45, so I've got plenty of time. I'm not really one for quotes and mottos, but six years on, I have a couple: 'If you're going to be bad, be confident. And if what you're doing is rubbish, at least try to be funny.' That motto served me well in Tampa and has done ever since.

* * *

When I played cricket, I was out of my comfort zone every day. Every time I went out to bat or came on to bowl, I didn't know what was going to happen. But I've never been further out of my comfort zone than when I was at school. The school I went to was on a rough estate and notorious in Preston. It was one of those schools that nobody wanted to go to, but I did, because it was just around the corner from my house, I didn't have to catch a bus and as soon as I was out of there at three o'clock, I could go and play cricket.

But because cricket was seen as a posh game for posh kids, my schoolmates thought I was a wrong 'un. Being different is never a good thing at school. I was like Billy Elliot, except cricket was my ballet dancing. I actually think it would have been easier being a ballet dancer – that lad had it easy. I was also pretty much a straight-A student – when I first started secondary school, teachers were talking about me going to Oxford or Cambridge – until cricket started getting serious.

I was an outsider, not one of the cool kids, a shy kid who barely spoke. It was only on the sports field that I came to life. Strangely, the fact that I played chess for Lancashire (my brother played for England) was acceptable, because some of the hardest kids at school played as well. One day you'd be involved in a life-or-death game of chess with one of the roughest kids in your class, the next he'd be trying to draw something rude on the back of your shirt. Looking back, it was quite an unusual place.

I played football to try to fit in. I was quite good at it, played for the oldest year in the school when I was only in the second year. I was big, played centre-half, and something happened to me when I went on the football pitch, as if I turned into a completely different animal. If we got beat, it was usually the goalkeeper's fault, but if it wasn't, the blame usually worked its way out from the back, so the centre-halves were next in the firing line. So nothing got past me, which won me some leeway with my would-be bullies. I was such an angry footballer, used to shout and scream at people and pick fights, because I knew the other kids had my back, and I suppose I was trying to impress them.

But off the pitch, it was a case of fight, run or hide. I mostly hid, fought when I absolutely had to, but never ran. I kept my head down and went about my business, but I never knew what was going to happen – whether I'd come home with my nose straight, my teeth intact or my shirt torn to shreds.

The bullies were usually small with an army behind them, which was the problem. None of them have been in contact since my cricket career took off, although I wish they would. I hate bullies, they're the worst kind of people. Even I feel a bit guilty that I bullied people on the cricket field. People say bullying is just part of professional sport, but that doesn't really make it right.

I was vocal on the field, but never abusive. Actually, there was one time. When we played India in the Twenty20 World Cup in 2007, my ankle had gone, I thought it was going to be my last game ever and I was in a very bad place. When Yuvraj Singh started hitting sixes all over the park, and being cocky with it, I threatened to wring his neck. He came down the pitch and started waving his bat at me. Next over, he hit Stuart Broad for six sixes. Every six he hit, he gave me a smile, and after the fourth, I was clapping.

Most of the time I used my size to intimidate the opposition, while trying not to be a dick. But my first Test against South Africa taught me that other teams played by a different moral code. They called me every name under the sun, there were C-bombs exploding all around me, it was awful. I looked around at these people and I wasn't upset, I was disappointed. I was 20 years old, I'd watched them on the telly, I liked and respected them. Now look at them.

Daryll Cullinan was meant to be religious, always talking about God, but he was the worst of the lot. That lad must say a lot of Hail Marys. I was in shock at what he came out with, thinking, 'Did he really just say what I thought he did?' I felt like saying, 'Come on, lads, I'm only trying to have a bat.' I mentioned it once in the press, and it got back to him. He did this interview accusing me of trying to make a name for myself. I thought, 'If I was trying to make a name for myself, I'd pick a player who people knew. Of all the names I could have chosen – Sachin Tendulkar, Brian Lara, Ricky Ponting, Jacques Kallis, Inzamam-ul-Haq – why would I choose someone as obscure as you?'

In comparison, most other countries were tame. Whenever I came out to bat, Pakistan fast bowler Shoaib Akhtar would call me 'fat boy' or 'chubby'. During the third Test in Lahore, I was walking to the middle, he started chirping, and I turned around and said, 'You know what, Shoaib? You look like Tarzan but bowl like Jane.' He put his run-up back by about ten yards, came charging in, let fly and splattered my stumps. As I was walking off, he shouted, 'Oi! Fatty!' I turned around and he started making that noise that Tarzan makes.

The Aussies were fine, aggressive but not abusive. When Shane Warne was chirping away, I'd be looking at his gleaming white teeth and fake tan and thinking, 'Mate, you bowl spin, you can't even hurt me.' Glenn McGrath was the world's worst sledger. He just shouted random expletives at you, as if he had Tourette's. And if you went back at him, he didn't know what to do. It was as if you'd scrambled his hard drive, he'd start looking round at his mates for someone to reboot him.

Glenn wasn't the brightest, but he was horrible to bat against, the only bowler who made me feel inadequate. He just bowled it where I couldn't hit it, and every time it did hit my bat I was relieved. The Aussies' intimidation came from them being good and knowing it. The verbals were just to put you off, distract you, make you question yourself. So there was no having a go at your mum or wife or anything along those lines. They were in your face, no doubt, but I can't remember ever walking off and thinking, 'That went too far.'

Other people might have had different experiences, and certainly Ian Bell copped it a bit in 2005. Then again, they were only calling him the Sherminator, from *American Pie*. That was actually quite funny, because they had a point. First time it happened, he came into the dressing room and said, 'They were calling me the Sherminator, what's that about?' I was thinking, 'Belly, have you looked in the mirror lately?'

I don't feel particularly unfortunate or special for being bullied at school, because it happened to pretty much everyone, even to some of the bullies. It was a rite of passage, and it just so happened that it was my turn to get bullied quite often. But it wasn't just at school where I didn't fit in. While the kids at school thought I was a weirdo because I played cricket, I didn't have anything in common with the middle-class kids I played cricket against either, because I was a wrong 'un from an estate. So I ended up floating around between different tribes. From the age of nine or ten I was playing men's cricket with my dad, but I didn't fit in with them either. I saw, heard and learned things I shouldn't have in dressing rooms and clubhouse bars, which didn't really tally with what was going on in the school playground.

I looked at some of the other kids doing drugs or robbing cars, and I didn't want to be like them. I remember getting into a car one night and realising it had been nicked. I got home and thought, 'You know what, that's not what I want to be doing and that's not who I want to be. I hate this.' But it takes a certain kind of strength to be your own person when you're just a kid.

It was an odd situation, but a great grounding. I was able to plough the lessons I learned from the tough times at school into everything I've done since. I wouldn't go back and change a thing, because it made me resilient, made me realise that if I'm passionate about something, even if everyone else thinks it's strange, I've got to cling on to it. That's my way out. Not fitting in at school is not necessarily a bad thing, it can be your salvation in the long term.

When Daryll Cullinan and his mates started abusing me in Nottingham, I thought, 'Lads, you really should have found out where I came from, and what I had to go through to get here. Say whatever you want, I'm really not arsed.' Nothing could have been as tough as some of the situations I'd been in. Being bowled a 90mph bouncer has more in common with being jumped by some kids on the way home from school than you might imagine.

Everything was beyond my control on the cricket field as well, regardless of how well I prepared and how good I was, but I enjoyed being out of my comfort zone in cricket. At school I spent a lot of time hiding, but there's no place to hide on the cricket field. If you try, you get buried. So I had to fight, and I learned to take the aggressive option. And while my ability to play a cover-drive or a pull or a hook doesn't really carry much weight outside of cricket, I was able to carry that aggression into the next part of my life.

CHAPTER 2

AT LEAST I'VE GOT A FUNNY STORY

A brief history of boxing

Not long after my trip to Florida, after changing management to focus on TV more, I made a documentary for the BBC about sportspeople and depression. One of the interviewees was Barry McGuigan, who killed an opponent in the ring and was still struggling to come to terms with the fact his brother had taken his own life a few years earlier.

We went down to Barry's house in Kent, met his son Shane, who was training Belfast's future world champion Carl Frampton, and after we'd done the interview I said to Barry, 'Can I just hit the pads with you holding them so I can tell my mates?' I hit the pads for a minute or so, and Barry said, 'You're actually all right, you've got a decent right hand.'

Barry shared the same management company as me, and about a month later we just happened to be in the office at the same time, so I popped my head around the door and jokingly said, 'I've just had a meeting about having a fight...' Afterwards, we had a chat in the corridor and Barry said, 'Would you be up for it?' I really wasn't, but this was Barry McGuigan, British and Irish boxing legend, so I didn't want to say no.

I was winging it, but we pitched it to Sky as an alternative to the wrestling documentary, and they liked the idea. A few days later, Barry arranged for me to travel to Essex to get my head kicked in. The plan was for me to do five rounds of sparring, to see if I could take a punch. I seriously thought about feigning injury to get out of it but ended up in the ring with this lad called 'Biggy', a 21-stone Nigerian, who knocked me around for 15 minutes. My mouth was bleeding, my nose was bent, but I was still standing at the end of it. So Barry said, 'Yeah, I reckon we can do this', and put together a three-month training schedule.

I was 18-and-a-half stone, so had to lose weight and get fitter, and while I enjoyed the training, not least because I'd always wanted abs, the actual boxing was horrific. I'd never done any boxing, and the McGuigans weren't really interested in schooling me in the finer points of the game. Other than a little bit of technical advice on the pads, their approach was to chuck me in at the deep end and see what happened, which meant that every spar I had was a fight.

I turned up at Aldershot army barracks, loads of squaddies were in the gym, and while none of them were heavyweights, they could all box a bit. I got speaking to one lad from Manchester and thought he seemed like a decent bloke. He was from my neck of the woods, we seemed to get on well, so I thought he'd go easy on me. But just before the spar, he disappeared with his gloves, and the next time I saw him we were in the ring together. I looked at his gloves and thought, 'Hang on a second, they're not the ones he was wearing before.'

Shane sent me out for the first round and when this fella hit me in the face, I could feel his knuckles. After the first round, my head was aching and the bones in my face were hurting, and Shane said, 'He's done us here, he's taken the padding out of his gloves.'

'Let's go home then.'

'We can't, it's all about image and saving face.'

'I'm not bothered about that, he's going to kick my head in.'

'No, you've got to do your five rounds...'

So I did my five rounds, got my head kicked in, and afterwards I had this headache that just wouldn't go away. The following day, I played in a charity cricket match in Sheffield, and my mate Mungo, who was the cameraman for the documentary, said, 'Are you all right, mate?'

I replied, 'No, I'm not, my head really hurts.'

I was in bits, properly broken, had never felt anything like it.

I also went to the Peacock Gym in East London, which has hosted some of Britain's best boxers. I fought a lad there who claimed he'd had 40-odd unlicensed fights and had 'ASSASSIN' tattooed on his chest in three-inch-high red lettering. He was the only person I wanted to hurt in a ring. For all his talk, he wasn't very good, and at one point I had one glove behind his head and was punching the shit out of him with the other one. That felt good.

Another sparring partner was a six foot ten Ukrainian, who wasn't quite as good as Vitali Klitschko but who kept making me miss by about two feet. At Shane's gym in Battersea, I sparred this frightfully posh rugby player who worked in IT and had done a bit of Muay Thai. I hit him with a short right hook, his legs started wobbling and Barry started shouting, 'Get in there! Finish the job!' Instead, I stopped boxing and said, 'Sorry, mate, are you all right?' I didn't want to finish him, I just felt bad at having hurt him in the first place. He was a nice lad who had taken the afternoon off work to come and have a spar, why would I want to knock him out? Barry wasn't very impressed, but he wasn't the one in the ring.

This was very deep water I found myself in, well above my head. Some days I swam, some days I sank. It got to the point where I was driving from my home in Surrey to the Peacock, and the journey would get slower and slower, because I didn't really want to arrive.

One morning, I turned up late, the six foot ten Ukrainian had to leave, and I thought, 'That's no bad thing.' But then this other lad asked to spar me, who was about 250 pounds of pure muscle, as nice as pie, but with a reputation for banging people out in the gym. He absolutely destroyed me. At one point, I saw this right hand coming at me, ducked, and he hit me on the top of the head, so that it went back into my neck, as if I was a cartoon tortoise. When it popped out again, I sprang back into my corner and he beat ten bells of shit out of me. It felt like I had whiplash, so I instinctively took a knee before telling Shane I was done.

The day had been a real struggle even before that, and there's nothing worse than getting in a boxing ring when your head's not right. I felt depressed, but Shane didn't know that and wasn't happy about me wanting to call it a day. On the cricket field, I could still bowl when I had all those negative feelings, but I was highly unlikely to get badly hurt playing cricket. Yet here I was, jaded before I even got into the ring, getting battered into a state of ever-increasing numbness. That was the only sequence that didn't make it into the documentary. It was messy, I looked terrible, and I don't think anyone wanted to see me like that. Except maybe Daryll Cullinan.

A week before D-Day, they told me I was going to fight some American lad called Richard Dawson at the Manchester Arena. They said they'd been scouring the world for an opponent, as if I was Apollo Creed in *Rocky*, and now they'd finally found one. I'd never heard of him. I didn't really want to know anything about him anyway. Unless it was the same Richard Dawson who used to bowl spin for Yorkshire and England, I wasn't interested.

Whoever they'd managed to dredge up, I'd have felt miles out of my depth. I started questioning everything. I kept seeing these posters of me all over Manchester and there were 10,000 people coming to watch: this was a ridiculous situation I'd landed myself in.

About five days before the fight, the day before I was meant to be heading to Manchester for the final part of the training camp, I found myself sitting at the top of a staircase in my flat, thinking, 'I'm not a boxer, all I wanted was a new house with a nice kitchen. I want to get out of this... I really want to get out of this... How the hell do I get out of this?'

Then I thought, 'Why not throw yourself down the stairs and try to break your ankle?' It was like that scene in *Escape to Victory* when they break the goalkeepers arm. I knew my right ankle was a bit dodgy anyway, so I stood up, took a deep breath ... and bottled it.

However far out of my comfort zone I've roamed, I've always been able to see the funny side. In fact, the more ridiculous the situation I find myself in, the funnier I find it. There's a line in the sitcom *Peep Show*, when Mark gets himself into yet another absurd predicament, and Jez says to him, 'At least you've got a funny story to tell.' That's how I felt when I was standing in that ring in Tampa, having a go at everyone, or sat in the doctor's office, with two broken ribs. And that's how I felt, sitting at the top of the stairs, contemplating doing myself an injury, to get out of this bloody fight I'd got myself into.

A few days before the fight, Mungo asked how I was bearing up, and I told him that I was shitting myself. He replied, 'The only advice I can give you is to play the part of a boxer.' I thought, 'Yeah, there's something in that.' When I was a cricketer, I played the role of this ultra-confident person: I wouldn't take a backward step; I seemed bulletproof. I never actually felt like that, but I convinced everybody else that I did, which is a powerful trick. So I thought, 'Mungo's right, maybe I can turn myself into a similar animal in the boxing ring?'

I started getting a bit of a swagger, walking around Manchester as if I owned the place. Then I saw Ricky Hatton, whose gym I was using for final preparations. Ricky had just lost a comeback fight and he looked like he'd been fed through a threshing machine. That took a bit of the spring out of my step.

The McGuigans got hold of some footage of Richard Dawson, who hailed from Oklahoma and had two wins from two professional fights, but I didn't watch it. Why would I want to see my opponent beating the shit out of somebody a few days before I climb in the ring with him? The first time I clapped eyes on him was at the press conference, which was the weirdest thing ever. It was at the Hilton in Manchester, and I turned up in a pair of tracksuit trousers and Timberland boots, to add a bit of height. It looked like I'd come straight from the building site, all I was missing was a hard hat.

I sat at this long table, with Jim Rosenthal, the compère, in the middle, and some fella with a big hat next to him, who I assumed was my opponent's manager. And next to him was sat 'Big Bad' Richard Dawson. To my dismay, 'Big Bad' Richard Dawson actually looked very big and very bad.

A journalist asked Dawson to tell us about himself. 'Well, I've been shot four times, I've been inside for GBH and I'm a debt collector by day.' I was thinking, 'For fuck's sake, really? Really, Barry? Of all the boxers in all the world, this is who you've come up with for my first fight? I thought boxing was all about match-making, surely you could have found some fat bouncer in Stoke?' Then a journalist asked me about my background. 'Well, I played cricket. We dress in whites and stop every two hours for a sandwich and a cup of tea. Oh, and I used to play a bit of chess...'

Barry had given me all this advice about what to do during the face-off, stuff like don't turn away first, make him look away. So I was looking down on him, staring straight into his eyes, as hard as I could, and all the time I was thinking, 'Please turn away, please turn away, I can't do this for much longer...' Eventually, he turned away to look at the cameras, and I was thinking, 'Well, maybe that's one point to me.' At least Barry seemed to think so.

I left the press conference in a state of confusion, not knowing if it had gone well or not, and when I returned to my hotel, I met up with my old England teammates Steve Harmison and Rob Key in the bar. They were looking at me, with pints in their hands, and suddenly Keysey said, 'You all right, Trev?' (He always calls me Trev, I don't really know why.)

'Yeah, I'm all right, Keysey.'

'Bloody 'ell, Trev, 'ave you seen 'im? 'E's been shot four times, 'e's gonna kill ya.'

'Cheers, Keysey, that's all I need...'

Keysey is one of the funniest people I know, dry as a bone, but this was not the place nor the time to be around any negativity. I left him and Harmy fantasising about the many different ways I might meet my end, and retreated to my room to finally watch the footage of 'Big Bad' Dawson.

I know nothing about the technicalities of boxing, and never will. When I watch boxing, I rely on the commentators to tell me what's going on. But as I was watching, I was thinking, 'When he comes forward he's all right, but if you go at him he shits himself.' So I decided that the game plan would be to throw as many punches as I could in eight minutes.

The following day was the weigh-in, at which I decided to wear a pair of Union Jack boxer shorts, which made me look like I was in the BNP. Bad undies aside, I was looking good, had abs and everything, but I'd ended up losing too much weight, so was only 15-and-a-half stone on the scales, 25 pounds lighter than Dawson, which worried me a bit. Denton Vassell was defending his Commonwealth welterweight title on the same bill, and after he got off the scales he did this pose, which made all his muscles pop out. I decided to do the same, except when I did it, it looked like I was straining to do a shit.

* * *

The day of the fight. I had barely slept at all that night, but suddenly I'm in the car on the way to the arena, and everything's real. In the dressing room, I can hear the noise from the arena as other fights play out. I meet my cuts man, Ian 'Jumbo' Johnson, who I hope I don't need, and try to play it cool as proper boxing people who know the drill mill about.

Then the door bursts open and in falls my brother, who's been boozing all day with Darren Gough, another former England teammate. My brother is as pissed as ten men. 'Have you seen him?' he shouts. 'He's from the mean streets of America and he's fucking massive! He's gonna belt ya! He's gonna do to you what I've wanted to do for years!'

I turn to Barry and say, 'Can someone get rid of him?'

Goughie just stands there, laughing.

I get my hands wrapped and the drug testers come in, which I take as a compliment – 'They must think I'm all right if they're bothering to test me.' My cup and gloves are on, which are all taped up, so I say, 'I know the drill, you're not going to leave until I've given you a sample, but how are we gonna do this?' So this bloke grabs the pot, we head to the toilet and I think, 'Fuck it, I'm gonna have some fun with this fella.'

I'm standing at the urinal and I say, 'Mate, you're gonna have to pull me pants down...'

'What?'

'Well, I can't do it, I've got gloves on. Why can't you pull them down for me?'

'I'm not pulling them down.'

'Well, someone's gonna have to pull me pants down.'

Eventually, one of my team caves in and pulls them down, and I'm stood there with my gloves by my side.

'Any chance you can hold it as well?'

'I'm not holding it.'

So I say to the drugs fella, 'Can you put your rubber glove on and hold it?'

'No!'

'Well, just put the pot down there and I'll aim for it, see what I can do...'

Urine collected, Shane gets the pads out and wants me to warm up. I was never really into warming up in cricket, always thought it used up precious energy, so I just throw a few punches out there. Shane is getting pissed off, so I say, 'Don't worry, Shane, I'm saving it', as if I have some idea of what I'm doing.

So I'm standing behind the curtain waiting to be introduced, wearing a Lancashire cricket shirt. The music kicks in – Oasis, 'Roll with It' – and the place goes off. As I walk through the curtain, something happens. I've been nervous and on edge, but suddenly I feel focused. By the time I'm in the ring, I'm thinking, 'This is amazing, I'm having this.' Shane and Barry are giving me a pep talk, but I'm in a world of my own. I look around the arena, can see all my mates ringside, and I say to myself, 'I can't embarrass myself in front of this lot, I'm gonna destroy this bloke.'

I start off all right, throw out a couple of jabs, but suddenly lose everything – any technique I'd picked up, my shape, my discipline and very nearly my dignity. I'm windmilling, swinging from every angle, because I'm so desperate to knock him out, and then, in the second round, I find myself on the canvas. One second I'm standing up, the next second I'm on the floor. I didn't feel a punch. After popping straight up again I'm standing there thinking, 'What happened there?' I can see all my mates laughing – Keysey, Harmy, Goughie, my brother more than any of them. My mum is crying, my missus is shouting and screaming, and I think, 'I'm gonna have to get up and win this fight now, otherwise I'll never hear the last of it...'

* * *

I did get up, and ended up winning on points. The scorecards differed, which wasn't ideal. I didn't get many clean shots on him either, I was mainly chucking him about, but I felt I deserved the victory.

What I hadn't told anyone was that a few weeks before the fight I injured my shoulder so I couldn't use my right hand properly. Then, during the third round, I felt it go completely, and by the end I couldn't lift my right arm up at all. That night, I did the press conference, put my tracksuit back on, put a big coat over the top and put my hand in the pocket. But when I tried to take it out again, I couldn't. There was something badly wrong, but I didn't want to ruin the night.

I hadn't had a drink for three months, and they said I wasn't allowed one at the after-party, because if I suffered a bleed on the brain, they wouldn't be able to do anything about it. Worse, I still couldn't pick my arm up, so I asked my missus to phone Dave 'Rooster' Roberts, my faithful old physio from my cricket days. Rooster told me my arm had become detached from my shoulder, so I went to see a specialist, had it scanned, and they micro-fractured it in order to regenerate it. It was an injury that turned out to be a blessing. Towards the end of the training camp, I'd almost decided to try to play cricket again because I'd felt so light and fit. I was thinking, 'If I can box, maybe I can bowl?' But there was no way on earth I'd be able to bowl after surgery on my shoulder.

I'd wanted that six-pack for years, but now I looked at it in the mirror and thought, 'I've done that. What next?' Every time I'd crawled to the top in my life, that feeling of elation was very short-lived before I fell off the cliff and went crashing into the waves again. I had the same feeling after I won anything at cricket. The enjoyment came from the achievement, the challenge, the getting there. Once it was all over, I wanted to start again. Being out of your comfort zone is a good place to be, and being too cosy is not for me.

CHAPTER 3

WHAT'S THE WORST THAT CAN HAPPEN?

Having a go

When I was a kid, nothing I ever did was good enough, whether I was playing well or playing badly. It meant I never stopped working to improve, but it was also exhausting. It's also a big part of the reason my head is in the state it's in now, because no matter what I do, whether it's a musical or a gameshow or a podcast, I always think I could have done it better. But my overriding feeling is, 'What's the worst that can happen? And who cares anyway?' Whether it's a gameshow, a podcast or a musical, I'm not solving world peace. I'm just here to entertain, do a bit of singing and dancing, that's all. I'm not performing complex heart surgery. Whether it all goes right or it all goes wrong, after I've finished I'm going to get in the car and drive home to my family, who are the most important people in my world.

If I have a life philosophy, it's 'have a go'. I'm pretty sure that's what *carpe diem* means in Latin. I have no fear of trying anything, but I do have a fear of not trying. Imagine getting to 60 and thinking, 'I wish I'd done that; what if I'd done this?' I'd rather have a go and fail than not try at all. It would be unfair to my management team to suggest there is no plan, but my plan is basically do as much as I can.

Believe it or not, my original plan (in my head at least) was to box David Haye, not 'Big Bad' Richard Dawson. It didn't matter that Haye had only just lost his world heavyweight title to Wladimir Klitschko, that was honestly my goal. When Haye was a guest on *A League of Their Own*, he had beaten Jack Whitehall up, which I thought was disgusting. As you know, I hate bullies. The segment was meant to be a bit of fun, but they put Jack inside a heavy bag and Haye hammered him, even hit him in the head at one point. I was sat there fantasising about fighting him. He would have killed me, but I would have had a bloody good go.

When I boxed, there was a lot of criticism in the media. People thought I was taking the piss out of the sport. It was actually the opposite: I wanted to show how hard it is. And apart from that one day when I got my head kicked in at the gym, nothing was off limits to the cameras. I was totally honest, because I wanted to celebrate boxers, not demean them. So I wasn't bothered about the criticism. I don't believe in people not being able to do things. I truly believe anyone can do anything within reason. The only person who holds you back is yourself. When people say they can't do something, I just don't understand it.

One reason people don't do things is because they're afraid of looking stupid or uncool. At my school, if you kept putting your hand up to answer questions, you'd get your head kicked in, because it was unfashionable to be clever. And I think that must have happened to a lot of people, because so many adults think in a similar way. They don't want to put their hands up to do something in case they get ridiculed. You will look stupid, more than once, but one day you won't. And who'll be laughing then?

I think I frustrate people with my attitude, piss people off, because I'm always telling them that they can have it all. That's not something people necessarily want to hear because it blows all their excuses out of the water. And giving anything a go doesn't always go down too well with the people closest to you. Before my one and only boxing match, my mum came to visit for the weekend. I'd mentioned I was thinking about stepping in a ring but hadn't confirmed anything. We happened to be watching some boxing on the telly, and she turned to me and said, 'Andrew, I'm so pleased you didn't decide to do that.' The bout had already been arranged, so I turned to her and said, 'Mum, I've got something I need to tell you...' My poor mum was gutted.

But you can't go through life acting on the advice of others, otherwise you'd never do anything. I wasn't the best cricketer by any stretch, there were people a lot better than me, but I desperately wanted to do it for a living, practised hard and found a way. I reckon if I'd been a young lad who wanted to be a footballer, I'd have been a footballer. I didn't love football like I loved cricket, but all it is is kicking a ball, just as all cricket is is hitting, throwing and catching a ball. Your genes obviously help, but they're only part of the story.

I didn't have a natural fast bowler's build, I was too big, which is why I used to get injured. I didn't bowl for eight years as a kid because of a bad back, so I was only ever meant to be a batsman. And my bowling action was terrible. I'd look at people I played with and be so jealous of them. Steve Harmison had a lovely action, Jimmy Anderson's is beautiful, but, with me, everything was an effort. As I was running in to bowl, I'd be thinking, 'This is absolute poetry...' But when I watched it back, I was all arms and legs, and it looked like my shoelaces were tied together. But eventually I got to a point where I thought,

'I don't care where my arms and legs go, as long as the ball goes where I want it to.'

I wasn't very good at boxing, but I had a professional fight. I beat an actual boxer, from a standing start. All because I thought, 'Why not have a go?' If you want to box, learn how to box, then box. If you want to act, learn how to act, then act. If you want to be a poet, learn how to write poems, then write poems. Everything is there for you, if you want it enough.

I've not taken easy options, but having gone out on limbs, there were always people wanting me to come crashing back to earth. Rob Key always says to me, 'When you fall flat on your face, I want to be there to see it.' The difference is, he's a mate and he's only joking. But there are people I played with and against, people I worked with, members of the public, the press, who would love to see me fail. I like that, it spurs me on. It's no different from when I was a cricketer: write me off and I'm confident I'll make you look stupid.

It annoys me when people say I'm lucky or have been given everything. They think I swan around, getting gigs for no other reason than I used to be Freddie Flintoff the cricketer. But there are so many people who have had successful sporting careers and done nothing afterwards. I've worked my arse off, practised hard, put the hours in. It annoys people if you step into 'their' world and upset the applecart. Fine, I didn't go to drama school or whatever school I should have gone to, but I've done plenty of catching up and carved out opportunities for myself. People don't see me at the BBC learning how to present, or taking acting and singing lessons and dying on my arse, or getting up early to write sitcoms or stand-up routines. I guess it's a lot easier for people to think I've been handed everything on a plate.

Everything I've said I wanted to do, I've done, and I've not turned down many things that really appealed to me. I wish I'd been a bit more like I am now when I was playing cricket. I was fearless to a degree on the cricket field, but if I played now I'd be even more gung-ho. It's the only way to be. What's the worst that can happen? That phrase has become a bit of a mantra of mine. Seriously, what's the worst that can happen if you give something your best shot?

I've got a mischievous side and like to shock. Not just other people, me as well. I always put myself in situations where I'm not sure what the outcome is going to be, where I'm not sure if I can pull it off. I love that feeling of not knowing what I'm getting myself into. Nothing is going to come close to the buzz that cricket gave me, but the closest buzz I can get now is throwing myself into things that are quite likely to sink me. The number of times I've been in a meeting, discussing a potential new work project, and found myself thinking, 'How have I ended up here?

This is just daft.' But instead of making my excuses, getting up and walking out, I'll have a little chuckle instead.

I'd love to play cricket again, it was my dream job. But, that aside, I've never been happier and more comfortable in myself. And although it might sound strange, the fact I feel so comfortable means I'm happier to roam from my comfort zone. So when I was approached to perform in a musical, my reaction was, 'Yeah, why not. What's the worst that can happen?'

I got a taste of the stage when I hosted a show for ITV called *All Star Musicals*, which involved seven famous people who had always wanted to do musical theatre getting a chance to perform at the London Palladium. Michael Crawford – *Barnum*, *Phantom of the Opera*, Frank Spencer – was a judge and mentor, and I had to rehearse my opening number while he was watching from the wings.

Of course I was nervous because I was a fish out of water. I was surrounded by all these musical theatre folk who had been singing and dancing their whole lives, so I felt very vulnerable and insecure. But I knew that feeling well, so was able to control it. When I was playing cricket, I'd get scared a lot. I tell people I have no fear of failure, but I do. Nobody wants to fail, so anybody who says they've got no fear of failure is a liar. I was nervous before every game I played, before I came on to bowl, especially before I came out to bat. Nobody would have known, because I'd be sitting on the balcony in my pads, drinking a cup of tea. But I promise you I was.

The only reason people think feeling nervous is bad is because they've been told it is. In most people's minds, nerves are horrible, a negative, destructive phenomenon. But when I played cricket, I revelled in nerves. I liked standing there in the middle, with the bowler sprinting towards me and that sensation of not knowing what was going to happen next. The nerves made me move faster, feel more focused, more energised, more alive. The reason you play sport is to be involved in those big moments. Even now when I watch sport I get a bit jealous. I'll watch someone take a penalty in a big match and think, 'I wish that was me.'

When I started doing *A League of Their Own*, I'd drink before I went on, to overcome the nerves, and it became the norm in most of the things I did. I got the dosage wrong a couple of times and didn't really know what was going on, which isn't great when James Corden and Jack Whitehall are whistling jokes past your head at 100mph. But now I'm a non-drinker, I've learned to just get on with things. So when the time came to perform my number at the Palladium in front of 2,000 people and Michael Crawford, I had that tingly, nervous feeling again. I loved not knowing if I was going to fluff my autocue, fluff my lines, sing out of tune, get some dance steps wrong. It was the same feeling I get when I do live stuff on TV. I won't know what I'm going to say, my heart will be pounding, but as soon as I'm on, something just clicks.

I still question myself a lot. I find myself in positions, with work or socially, where I think I'm not going to be able to do it. The number of times I've been out onstage or doing a TV show and thinking, 'I'm not sure I've got this in me, I genuinely don't know if I can do this.' But if I'm not doubting myself, I'm in the wrong job.

I met Kay Mellor at a casting for her drama series, *Love, Lies and Records*, and landed a part in one of the episodes. She thought I could do a job in her musical adaptation of *Fat Friends*, which was a big TV hit in the early 2000s and starred, among many other now-famous names, James Corden. Kay cast me as Kevin Murgatroyd, the slightly dopey fiancé of the lead character, which took a leap of faith on her part, because while she might have suspected I was slightly dopey, she had no idea if I could perform onstage.

I was far more nervous doing musical theatre than I was doing boxing. I turned up for the first day of rehearsals and that same old thought came back again: 'What am I doing? Why am I here?' The first thing we did was gather around the piano and have a sing-song, and I was just moving my mouth, so that nothing was coming out. Everyone else was having a little contest among themselves, seeing who was the loudest and the best, and to say I felt inadequate would be putting it mildly. But I had a little chuckle, began to feed off the nerves and, before I knew it, I'd pulled myself together.

You know when you watch a musical and it feels a bit embarrassing when someone starts singing, well, now imagine being that person who has to start singing. But I thought, 'It doesn't matter how much I practise, I'm never going to be as good as most of them, I can only be as good as I can possibly be.' Once I'd sung in front of them for the first time, I realised I enjoyed it. It's like swimming with sharks: you're floating about in a cage, and you've been told that the sharks aren't going to attack you, but you're still thinking, 'This is absolute madness.' But the sharks don't attack and it ends up being one of the best things you've ever done.

I didn't just want to get it right for me, I wanted to get it right for Kay, because she had shown so much faith in me, as had Nick Lloyd Webber, the son of Andrew, who had written the music. If someone puts faith in me, I give it back tenfold. It was the same when I played cricket. I didn't want a coach telling me how I should bat or bowl, I just wanted to play for someone who backed me 100 per cent. Obviously, I needed a few tips on acting and singing, but now that they'd thrown their weight behind me I knew I would improve.

I didn't really have any expectations of what my theatre colleagues were going to be like. I used to think, 'Cricket, sport, that's my world, that's my bread and butter, my meat and two veg, anyone who isn't into cricket or sport is a bit strange.' Professional sport is a very insular world, sportspeople think it's the only way to live. When you live in that world, you think you have to stick with the same group of mates and behave in a certain kind of way until your dying day. It's such a narrow way of thinking.

When I retired from cricket, it dawned on me that I'd missed out on knowing so many interesting people. There I was hitting and throwing a ball about for all those years, thinking it was the only show in town and that these were 'my people', sod all the rest, and there was actually a bigger, wider world out there in need of exploring. Now, I don't care what walk of life someone is from – wrong 'uns are wrong 'uns, whether they play cricket or work behind the counter in Greggs. In the same vein, good people are good people, end of story.

I'm friends with a lot more women now, gay people, people who have no interest in sport and barely know what cricket is. So I got on with the main players in the musical really well, they all knew my background and could not have been more welcoming and supportive. Jodie is from Blackpool, just down the road from me. Sam Bailey was a prison officer before she won *The X Factor*. Kevin Kennedy, who played Curly Watts on *Coronation Street*, has lived a life outside of the acting game – he was even a member of the Smiths, before Morrissey joined and they became the Smiths. My understudy was a fella called Joel Montague, who was absolutely amazing. I felt a bit bad, because he'd just finished playing the main role in *School of Rock* in the West End. He'd won awards and accolades, so I thought he might be a bit resentful towards me. But he was lovely, helped me a lot.

I did get few scathing looks, because noses had been put out of joint. If I fluffed a line slightly in rehearsals, I'd see hands go over mouths, presumably because they were moaning about me. I get it: they've been to drama school and as far as they're concerned, some bloke who played cricket has popped into their world and been given a plum role, including a few songs. But that's life, and I don't feel bad about it. I cast for it, gave it everything I had, and landed the part.

And I'd also think, 'You know what, they booked me because they wanted me.' I'm not going to make any bones about it, I knew why I was there: to attract people to the show who don't normally go to the theatre. So I wasn't bothered, I found it funny and it lit a fire under me.

Matthew Syed – who's one-third of our BBC 5 live podcast, the other being Robbie Savage – once said that it looked like

I winged everything, including the podcast. I'll be honest: I don't do a great deal of preparation for the podcast. But you can't get away with that in musical theatre. I had to learn scripts and how to sing, or at least how to hold a note, just as I practised bloody hard to get good at cricket. I noticed that some of the cast didn't want to see their notes after a performance because they didn't like criticism. But I wanted pages and pages of notes because I was desperate to improve.

At the premiere in Leeds, all I was thinking was, 'Me mum and dad are sat in the audience and I'm standing here in a boiler suit about to start singing.' My dad is a classic Northern man, he says exactly what he thinks. So, in the first scene, I had to fix this door, and I had to fix it properly, because otherwise I knew he'd be sat there thinking, 'He's not done that right.' I didn't seek them out during the show because I didn't want to be distracted, but I saw them at the end, when we were taking our bows, which was lovely.

My missus was also there, which was a little bit awkward, because I did this song with Jodie Prenger – who played my fiancée – which finished with a kiss. While I was kissing her – it wasn't an open-mouthed snog, with tongues flying everywhere, it was just a stage thing – I could hear Robbie Savage, a man uninhibited by the niceties of the theatre, shouting, 'Go on, Freddie!' Me and Jodie started giggling, and I whispered, 'Sorry about that, it's just my mate Robbie. He's an idiot...'

It definitely doesn't feel right, kissing someone else in front of your missus. But it could have been worse – I could have been doing *Strictly* (which Robbie did a few years back), where I'd be spending six hours a day with another woman, picking her up, throwing her upside down and sticking my nose in places it shouldn't really go.

The crowd in Manchester was mental. I started singing one song and people started laughing. I was thinking, 'You're not meant to laugh at this bit.' I was a bit thrown, lost my thread, got behind a bit and got stuck singing this note a bit too high. I sounded like a dying owl and had to pretend I'd got all emotional.

It was tough at times, because almost everyone else was a proper singer, while most of my singing experience was karaoke – usually after ten pints, sometimes in the Press Club, with my arm around Ricky Hatton – so I wasn't always in tune. But questioning yourself is never a bad thing. It's completely natural, and helpful, which is why I don't mind doing it. I've had imposter syndrome all my life, even with cricket. I question myself every day, but it's not the questions that are important, it's the answers you give. That's what makes me tick. If I'm not going to back myself to do something, I can't expect anyone else to. I've done a bit of treading water, but I've not sunk yet.

I'm not really into quotes, but there is one from former US president Theodore Roosevelt, from a speech he made, that sums my attitude up nicely:

> It is not the critic who counts; not the man who points out how the strong man stumbles, or where the doer of deeds could have done them better. The credit belongs to the man who is actually in the arena, whose face is marred by dust and sweat and blood; who strives valiantly; who errs, who comes short again and again, because there is no effort without error and shortcoming; but who does actually strive to do the deeds; who knows great enthusiasms, the great devotions; who spends himself in a worthy cause; who at the best knows in the end the triumph of high achievement, and who at the worst, if he fails, at least fails while daring greatly, so that his place shall never be with those cold and timid souls who neither know victory nor defeat.

I think I would have liked Theodore Roosevelt, he seemed like my kind of bloke. But most of the time, I kept the message simple. It's probably not what Kay Mellor wants to hear – or anyone who's worked with me or might in the future – but I got through the production with the thought, 'What's the worst that can happen?'

CHAPTER 4

MY OWN
WORST CRITIC

Not giving a shit

I was an easy target for the theatre critics, although I'm told most of the reviews were positive – Robbie used to read them out on the podcast. That said, calling me wooden was a bit lazy. If you're going to slate me, dig out a more original word than wooden.

During the run, I suddenly lost confidence in my singing. They changed my song a little bit, made it slightly higher, and no matter what I tried to do, I couldn't get it right. Leaders are important in any walk of life, because they're the people you can go to when you need a little bit of guidance or support. But my resident director, Craig, was ill and I really missed him. Usually when I sang well, the conductor would give me a wink or a thumbs-up. But now when I looked over, his head was buried in his music. I hadn't had that feeling in a long time. It was like running into bad form as a batsman. When you're in good nick, all you can see are gaps. When you're in bad nick, all you can see are fielders.

I have vivid memories of my failures on a cricket field, could tell you almost every way I got out since about the age of nine. If I could go back in time, I wouldn't relive the good bits, I'd want to fix those bits that went wrong. For the most part, I was a confident cricketer. I thought I was going to get Brian Lara out every time I bowled to him, even when he scored 400 against us. I thought the same with Sachin Tendulkar, who I regard as the best batsman who ever lived. I didn't just want to get him out for the good of the team, I also wanted to get him out to impress him. It's players like that who bring out the best in you. But before the 2005 Ashes, I'd never felt pressure like it.

We'd beaten everyone over the previous few years, the press were talking us up, they were talking me up, and it all got on top of me. When I bowled in the first Test at Lord's, my eyes were like saucers and I wasn't really in control. And when it was our turn to bat, I took a spot in the dressing room, overlooking the balcony, and was frozen to my chair. Usually, I'd be out the back, watching a bit of TV in my pants, having a laugh with Harmy. I couldn't make sense of it. I was thinking, 'All these people are here, me mum and dad are watching, we've not won the Ashes since 1987, I've got to bat against Glenn McGrath and Shane Warne, look at the size of that press box...'

When I walked out to bat, I usually felt alive – 'This is my stage, this is where I want to be' – but not that day. I took guard, looked around the field, and it seemed like there were about 30 Australians. I felt completely impotent. McGrath bowled me for a duck and we lost the game by a landslide. I choked, there's no other way of putting it.

Afterwards, I took a week off, went down to Devon with the family and didn't touch a bat or a ball. While I was down there, I thought, 'What were you thinking? You do this for fun. You pride yourself on turning up at the big moments. Next time, play the game on your terms.'

Second Test at Edgbaston, the first bad ball Warne bowled, I was going to have a go at. He lobbed one up, I didn't properly commit, but it just beat mid-off and ran away for four. After that, I was up and running. If only I could travel back to that first Test at Lord's and tell myself it doesn't matter as much as I think it does.

I'd also go back to the last Test of that series at the Oval. I was in the form of my life, thought I could do anything, had just hit Shane Warne straight back over his head for six, and then I popped one up for a caught and bowled. Kevin Pietersen came in, finished it off and we regained the Ashes, but that was the biggest moment in that series and I didn't come through it. That's my overriding memory of that day, not regaining the Ashes after 18 years, but getting out. I still close my eyes now and see that ball coming out of Warne's hand. I'll be in bed, struggling to sleep, and I won't be thinking about winning Sports Personality or World Player of the Year, I'll be thinking about the time I got out first ball against Pakistan – Danish Kaneria, fucking googly! Even now, I'll remember every line I fluff and every shit joke I tell, not things I've done well. The difference being, the memories don't pain me as much.

Because I'm my own worst critic, I couldn't have cared less what the actual critics thought about my performances. When I started playing for Lancashire and England, I didn't need to read about my performances in the newspapers. I already knew everything I needed to know – whether I played well or badly, won or lost. When people say they never read any of their press, they're lying. But I honestly didn't read much. And now, if I get any negative reaction on Twitter – and I'm lucky I don't get too much of it – I know it's coming anyway, because I've done something rubbish, like a bad TV show.

In the theatre world, everyone knows the critics, and when the reviews for *Fat Friends* started coming out, people would stick them up on the noticeboard, or you'd have actors thanking the critics on Twitter. That amazed me, because we were playing in front of packed audiences every night, they were standing on their feet at the end of every performance, clapping, cheering and looking happy. Everyone who had paid to come and see us loved it, but some people were hanging on one person's opinion. Who cares? I was performing in *Fat Friends* for me, for everyone else in the production and for the people who paid to watch. What could I do about any bad reviews anyway? I knew I could barely sing, so I just had to learn my lines and try my best every time I went out there.

In any walk of life, the most important things are what you can offer and whether you give it your all. If you spend too much time – or any time – worrying about what and how other people think, you'll end up in a state of paralysis. That's why I hated team meetings about the opposition. I'd be sat in a room with all my teammates and the coaches would be going through what the other team can do – where you should bowl to certain players, where they can score, where they can't score – and I'd be thinking, 'What's the point of this?' It would bore me to tears. I knew what Ricky Ponting could and couldn't do, but I didn't want to sit there talking about that. What's important is what I can do.

When it came to batting, I just tried to hit it. In terms of bowling, my good ball was my good ball, that's why I was in the team. It didn't matter if it was a tail-ender or Ricky Ponting, I just tried to hit the top of off-stump. If it nipped away, I might get an edge. If it nipped back, I might bowl you. You could show me every video under the sun and dissect everybody's technique, but it didn't change my approach. Glenn McGrath used to say he targeted individual batters. Bollocks he did, he just used to put the ball in exactly the same place every time, at 80mph. It was all just mind games.

I was the same, more interested in what I could do than the fella standing down the other end. I'm not sure I could ever be an England coach because of my reputation. Then again, that's nonsense. If I want to do it, I'll go and do it. And if I was England coach, I'd talk about us, our strengths, what we can do to win, what we can do to identify when something's not right with a teammate, and how we might be able to help him. It's no different to musical theatre. Kay Mellor didn't sit me down and say, 'Right, this is what the critics or crowd want you to do', she just wanted me to go out there and be me.

CHAPTER 5

FLOUNDERING WITH HARRISON FORD

The advantages of interloping

When I retired from cricket, a couple of journalists wrote articles suggesting I was floundering, groping around in the dark for a new identity. Did I feel a bit lost? Yes. When you retire from sport, your life changes dramatically. Playing cricket was the only thing I'd known since I was a kid and the only thing I'd ever wanted to do, but now I couldn't do it. When I hung up my bat, I spent a lot of time wondering what I was going to do. Who – and what – on earth was I? Of course, I questioned a lot of things about myself. Now, despite seeing where I could have done better, I look back on my career with fondness, at how lucky I was, which makes life easier. But when I retired, I couldn't help thinking that I could have played for longer and had been robbed of a chunk of my career. But it's how you recover from setbacks that's important, what you do next, and how successful you try to make it.

I was 31 but felt like I was 16 again, trying to carve out a different living. I was unsure of myself, not knowing if I belonged. When I played cricket, I hated routine, rebelled against it, but when I retired I quickly realised that routine was exactly what I needed, to keep me from drifting. But to say I was bumbling through life simply wasn't true. When I finished playing cricket, I decided that I didn't want to coach or be a commentator, like so many former cricketers before me. It would have been easy for me to become a pundit and talk about what I knew. But I like talking about cricket on my own terms, and I reckon doing it for a living would have been like pulling teeth. I wanted to see what else was out there. And that has meant ending up in situations that other people have found difficult to accept or understand.

I look at some of my friends and I envy them, because they have a nine-to-five job, live for the weekend when they go and get smashed, and head back to work on the Monday. There's nothing wrong with that, because they're happy. People think that if you 'settle' for that kind of life and aren't bothered about getting a better-paid job or working your way up the career ladder, there's something wrong with you. But I'd love to be like that, to be able to look around and think, 'You know what, I'm happy with life, this is all I need and it's brilliant.' But I can't do that, it doesn't appeal to me. If I'm not working towards something, I get fed up, because I feel like I'm standing still. If life isn't a challenge, I'm not alive. At times it's exhausting, but it's the way I have to be.

I did a few bits and pieces in front of the camera while I was still playing, some presenting on Sky, got work with ITV4 before being offered the gig on *A League of Their Own*. I'd be doing my management agency a disservice by saying I stumbled into anything, because they have a strategy. And I've not done anything I didn't want to do. So if I'm floundering, I'm a bloody good flounderer. I'm floundering with the best of them.

After my knee operation, I was told I'd never run again. But I took that as a challenge. I rang the surgeon up, told him I was running a bit, and he told me that if I could deal with the pain, I should crack on. So in 2014, I came out of retirement to play a few Twenty20 games for Lancashire. I knew I wasn't going to be anywhere near as good as I used to be, but I took a few wickets and scored a few runs in the final and ended up being signed by Brisbane Heat for the 2014–15 Big Bash competition. I loved it, but was rubbish, completely out of my depth because I could barely move. I felt bad, because Brisbane's coach, my old Lancashire teammate Stuart Law, had put a lot of faith in me and I didn't repay it on the field (although they did end up selling more tickets).

I also commentated on a few games while I was playing, with an on-field microphone, and sang Elvis's 'In the Ghetto' on the boundary when I was bored. That all went down well with the bosses at Network Ten, so they offered me a commentary role the following season and, as part of the deal, I was also offered a role on a live current affairs show called *The Project*. In Australia, they seem to think I'm intelligent, which is not a great reflection of the country. But the Aussies have always been very generous towards me, even when England were getting hammered on the cricket field. They accept flaws and failings, as long as you have a go.

Mind you, Aussies have gone soft. You can't cross the street unless there's a green man, otherwise you'll get done for jaywalking. You'll be standing there at the lights, there won't be a car within four miles, and they'll all be stood there like statues. If you do ignore the lights, people will tut and shake their heads. I was over there recently, trying to cross a road at about 3 a.m., and this lollipop woman started shouting at me and threatened to call the police. I was thinking, 'I've got this, I'm 40 years old, I don't need people ushering me across empty roads.' Everything is 'inappropriate' over there, so I spend a lot of time thinking, 'Why are you rolling your eyes at me?'

My ambition was never to be on TV, my ambition was to play cricket for Lancashire and England. If there's something exciting I want to do, I'll do it. But if it all goes wrong tomorrow, I can just go home and forget about it. That's a strangely liberating attitude. It frees you up, allows you to play shots you wouldn't otherwise play, instead of being like a rabbit in the headlights. So when *The Project* asked me to interview Will Smith and Margot Robbie in Los Angeles, I wasn't really fazed. Why would that bother me when I've faced Glenn McGrath and Shane Warne at Lord's in an Ashes Test match?

I caught a bus to the cinema to watch their film, got some popcorn, settled in, didn't like it, and left after half an hour. The following day, I didn't really know what I was turning up for, because I'd never done one of those press junkets before. I was sat in this waiting room with all the other journalists and got chatting to an English fella, who said to me, 'What are you doing here?'

'I don't really know.'

'What are you going to ask them?'

'I think I'm just gonna talk.'

'How long have you got?'

'Eight minutes.'

'Wow, you've done well, that's double time.'

My name gets called out, I walk down this corridor, plonk myself outside this room and this girl wanders over and says, 'Gerald is ready for you now.'

'Who's Gerald?'

'The gentleman you're interviewing.'

'To be honest, I'm just here for Will and Margot.'

'No, you've got to interview everyone...'

When I open the door, I've got no idea what's inside. I see this bloke sat there and recognise him as the older fella in the film, but I've still got no idea who he is. I sit down opposite him, say hello and ask what it was like working with Will Smith. His answer is unsettlingly brief. The film was about deceit and lying, I worked out that much, so I ask him whether it's easy to act in a film that's all about deceit and lying. Again, he keeps it economical, and it occurs to me that I've still got about six minutes left. Time to go off-piste.

I eye him up and down and realise he's dressed quite outdoorsy, in a check shirt, gilet, cargo trousers and boots, so I say to him, 'Do you like fishing?', and his eyes light up. Suddenly, Gerald is alive, telling me about the biggest fish he's caught on the fly and how all the world leaders should meet on a riverbank, fish together, bury hatchets and solve all the world's problems. He goes on for about five minutes, which would be great if we want it, but we don't want it, because the show's never going to use it, so it's just wasted air.

Gerald in the trash can, I'm ushered into another room, where I have to speak to some big bloke I don't know from Adam, called Adrian. I come straight out of the traps with, 'The film is about lying and deceit, is it ever acceptable to lie?'

'I could call you a fucking idiot right now and you wouldn't know if I was lying or being truthful.'

'I've got an idea, mate, but if this is how you want this interview to go, let's crack on, I can be like that as well.'

That was an awkward eight minutes.

Next it was Will Smith and Margot Robbie, which was a relief, because at least I'd seen Will in *The Fresh Prince of Bel-Air* and Margot in *Neighbours*. As I waited my turn, the room went into meltdown, because the girl before me tried to take a picture, and she was bundled out as if she was a selfie terrorist. When I walked in, I pushed a curtain open without realising it was part of the set, and it fell on top of Will and Margot. But I didn't really care, because they were just a man and a woman I didn't know but who happened to be famous.

Because I'd seen *Neighbours* more recently than *The Fresh Prince of Bel-Air*, I focused on Margot.

'What's it like working with Will Smith?'

'Yeah, it's fantastic...'

'But you've worked with all of the biggest actors in the world – Harold Bishop, Mrs Mangle, Toadfish...'

'Where are you from?'

'I'm English, but I work for an Australian programme called *The Project*. Heard of it?'

I don't think she's heard of it, but I plough on anyway.

'I was playing cricket in the Big Bash and ended up doing this. Bit strange really...'

Will Smith was looking left out and confused.

'One thing I've noticed since I've been in Australia is that the men have started taking very good care of themselves. They're all into grooming. That's not very Australian, is it? Look at Shane Warne, he promotes facial creams, wears a wig, whitens his teeth. Even Ricky Ponting has had a hair transplant.'

Margot was looking at me all puzzled and Will was sat there like a bookend. So I said to him, 'Will, are you into male grooming?'

'Hey man, black don't crack.'

'Would you contemplate having a hair transplant?'

He looked at me as if to say, 'Who is this fucking idiot?' before patting the top of his head. 'This ain't going nowhere, I've been tested.'

I sat there thinking, 'Easy, mate, it's fine, I was only joking', while the woman was gesturing for me to wrap things up. Strangely, neither Will nor Margot got in touch afterwards.

Mark Wahlberg was an absolute bellend. I watched *Ted 2*, which was even worse than *Ted 1*, texted Piers Morgan and asked if he had anything on him. Piers texted back and said, 'Great bloke, loves his cricket, he's thinking of getting involved in the Caribbean Premier League.'

I thought, 'Perfect, I'm on safe ground here, this will be a doddle. There's even a chance he might know me.'

He didn't, and he didn't seem to be that into cricket either, although Piers wasn't winding me up, he did have a stake in the Barbados Tridents.

I asked him a few cricket questions, but was getting nothing back, so I started asking him about his internet preferences and how often he deletes his history. After about two minutes of blankness, I said, 'Is there anything you want to tell me? About you? About *Ted 2*?'

He just looked at me as if to say, 'Be gone, fool', as if he was a king dismissing a jester from his throne room. I got up to shake his hand, and the girl stepped in and said, 'You've still got a minute and a half.' I looked at her and said, 'What's the point?'

I also interviewed Harrison Ford in Sydney when the new *Star Wars* film came out in Australia. I walked into the room, he was sat there, with the Harbour Bridge as a backdrop, and I was thinking, 'This is Harrison Ford, Han Solo, Indiana Jones, this is fucking brilliant!' I'd heard he could be a bit prickly, but I'd seen him on *The Graham Norton Show* with Jack Whitehall, and he seemed pretty relaxed on that. I mentioned Jack and Harrison broke into a smile and said, 'I love that guy, he's so funny.' I'd cracked him. So I started freestyling, asking him a load of daft questions about *Star Wars*.

'If you don't mind me saying, you've aged a bit, but Chewbacca still looks the same. How old is Chewie? And how long do Wookies live for?'

When I got back to Melbourne, they called me into the office and I thought I was in trouble for messing about.

The boss said, 'What did you say to Harrison Ford?'

'What do you mean? We had a great time, he loved it.'

'Yeah, I know, we've had an email from his office saying he's refusing to launch *Star Wars* tonight unless you ask the questions.'

'I can't go back to Sydney, I've just arrived in Melbourne.'

'Can you write your notes down then?'

'I didn't make any notes! If you want, I can write down on a piece of paper, "How old's a Wookie?"'

Harrison Ford had obviously been so bored out of his mind answering the same old questions that I'd struck a chord with him. It made me realise that coming at things from a different perspective and going off script can reap rewards, and that being seen as an interloper isn't necessarily a bad thing.

CHAPTER 6

A BIT OF BUMBLE

Notes on David Lloyd

I loved David Lloyd so much when I played cricket, and still do. He was just a brilliant man-manager. 'Bumble' signed me for Lancashire when I was 16. He came round to my mum and dad's, sat in the front room, drank from the best teapot, helped himself to the custard creams fanned out on a plate, and painted a picture of how it was going to be: 'We want Andrew to sign on a three-year contract and we'll start him off on £2,500 a year. It's onwards and upwards from there.' Bumble went on to explain the wage structure in some detail, said that Michael Atherton, who was England captain at the time, was being paid £28 grand a year by the county, and I was sat there thinking, 'Fucking hell, this is amazing. Pass me that pen!' The last words Bumble said to my mum and dad that day were, 'Don't worry, I'll look after him…'

When I turned up at Old Trafford for my first day of training, Bumble wandered up to me and said, 'Forget all that shit I told

yer mum and dad about me looking after yer, I'm gonna absolutely hammer yer.'

Bumble did hammer me, but he also looked after me, like
he looked after everyone. He took us on an England Under-19s
tour to the West Indies, and if anyone had a go at us – be it the
other team, the press, the crowd – he'd be the first to wade in
and fight for you. He was in the crowd in Guyana, and there
were about ten local fans shouting and screaming at us, so he
whipped out his teeth and offered all the fans out. Another
game, he marched on the pitch because the umpire had made
a few bad decisions. When the chairman tried to shoo him off,
Bumble turned round and said, 'Who the fuck are you? You
can have some as well!' To be fair to Bumble, he didn't know it
was the chairman, but he still got kicked out.

As a coach, Bumble wasn't brilliant at the technical side of
the game, but our relationship was more than player and coach.
He genuinely cared for me, so I would have done anything for
him and never wanted to let him down. One day, I was playing
for the second team against Yorkshire, got out, punched the
wall and had to have my hand pinned for eight weeks. Bumble
wasn't even the head coach, he'd moved on to England, but
was still around Old Trafford a lot. When he saw my hand in
a cast he said, 'Andrew' – he always called me Andrew, and
still does – 'what have you done?' I told him I'd punched a wall

after getting out, and all he said was, 'That was stupid, weren't it?' and walked off. That was far worse than any bollocking he could have given me.

So often in life you work with people who have their own agenda. We all do to some degree, because everyone wants to be successful in their own right. But I genuinely believe that my success meant as much to Bumble as it did to me. Bumble would tell me exactly what he thought of me, and that's the type of person I respond to best and try to emulate. Bob Simpson, the great Australian who also played for Lancashire, was the same. Early in my career, he sat me down in the dressing room at Old Trafford and unleashed on me. He told me I wasn't working hard enough, was underachieving, not fulfilling my potential. But I thought that was brilliant, because he was bang on the money and at least I now knew what I had to do. Another time it was my teammate Neil Fairbrother who gave me the mother of all bollockings. After that, we put a plan together to get back playing for England, and it worked. I don't understand why anyone wouldn't prefer that to getting no feedback at all.

What I didn't need was someone trying to coach me or interfere when I was playing well, or a dressing room of people patting me on the back or buying me drinks after I'd scored a hundred. I never understood that – it's not the lad who scored a hundred who needs a drink, it's the lad who scored no runs who needs looking after. I'm fine, I got a ton, he's not, he got nothing. That's when the coach earns his corn, when players are struggling. When a teammate was having a really bad run of form and really trying to make things better, I felt for them, although my empathy wasn't always reciprocated. You shouldn't wash your hands of them or drop players who are in a trough, although I played with a couple of coaches who were of that view.

Bumble played hard and took cricket very seriously, but he also saw it as fun. Once, I got hit in the nuts playing in Guernsey and when we came off for rain I was still doubled up in agony. He passed me a glass of water and said, 'Just put your balls in there.' So I'm sat there in the dressing room, with my balls in a pint pot, surrounded by my Lancashire heroes – Neil Fairbrother, Wasim Akram – and Bumble's giggling in the corner. Just as I put the glass down, Gary Yates walks in and says, 'Anybody got a drink?' Everyone looks at me and Bumble is gesturing towards the glass, with this wicked grin on his face. Quick as a flash I say, 'Here you go, Gary, get stuck in...'

I could write a whole book about Bumble. In his last game as Lancashire coach, we were playing at Derby, I got two ducks in one day and we got hammered. On the morning of the last day, we destroyed his clothes – slit his undies, cut the ends off his socks, pulled all the buttons off his shirt. The problem was, he used to go mad if we got beaten.

So we're all sat in the dressing room, trying to look sheepish, because we've just been taken to the cleaners, and he's going off on one. He's pointing to us one by one – 'You were fuckin' hopeless! And as for you!' – while he's trying to get dressed. He's pulling his undies up, and they've got no crotch, but he's still not stopping – 'And you, you fucker! Bloody useless!' When he pulls his socks on, his feet go right through them, but he's still going – 'And what kind of fuckin' shot was that?' The final straw is when he puts his shirt on, he's trying to do the buttons up and there aren't any. He stormed off after that. Turned out the shirt was a present from his missus.

Another time, I was touring Pakistan with England, and Bumble organised a quiz. Everyone was there – the media, the players – apart from Duncan Fletcher, the coach, which was weird, but not surprising. Me and Harmy turned up late, came last and got mocked by Bumble all night. We were presented with these mosque alarm clocks as booby prizes. So I said to Harmy, 'You and me are going to have some fun with these...'

We were staying in the same hotel, so I went to reception and got a key for Bumble's room. I set one of the alarm clocks for 2:30 a.m. and stuffed it behind his TV, set the other one for 4:30 a.m. and hid it behind his curtains, before disappearing from the scene of the crime, sharpish. Right on cue, we could hear this alarm clock going off – which was the very loud sound of people being called to prayer – and apparently Bumble was stumbling around his room in the dark, trying to turn the TV off, even though it wasn't even on. The noise woke the bloke in the next room, so he's knocking on Bumble's door and shouting. Bumble opens his door in his pants, starts shouting back at him and they nearly have a fight in the corridor. Bumble eventually finds the alarm clock, turns it off, goes back to sleep, and two hours later it all happens again.

I remember Bumble telling me, 'Don't do anything your mum wouldn't be proud of.' I've done a lot of things she definitely wasn't proud of, but he taught me so many other lessons that I took to heart and still heed to this day. Bumble practised what he preached, and if he thought I could do something, I'd throw the kitchen sink at it, give it everything. Just as if Kay Mellor thinks I've got it in me to play one of the lead roles in a musical she's written, and Nick Lloyd Webber thinks I can sing his songs, then I'll give it my best shot.

CHAPTER 7

ENJOYING GETTING PUNCHED

Dealing with depression

I'm not aggressive, in the sense that you won't find me fighting in the street, so boxing was playing against type. I felt terrible at times, travelling to the gym, knowing I was going to spar someone better than me. But the thought of getting beaten up was usually worse than the reality. There were times in training when I enjoyed getting punched. In fact, I enjoyed getting punched more than I enjoyed punching people. I'd take one on the chin and think, 'Come on then, let's have another one!' A psychologist might look at me and decide that I was a bit of a masochist. And they might be right.

When the injuries started during my cricket career, I enjoyed them. Strange as it sounds, I revelled in the pain, because it meant having to push myself as far as I possibly could. In fact,

I was playing through pain all the time, certainly in the latter part of my career. I'd be injected to the eyeballs, so that when I stepped on the pitch, I was playing against myself, more so than against the opposition. That was the main game for me, not the actual cricket. It didn't matter if I was bowling to Sachin Tendulkar or Ricky Ponting, it was my game, nobody else's. I was so proud every time I pulled on a Lancashire or England shirt, but everybody else on the pitch was just a pawn.

I never experienced pain in boxing as bad as I experienced in cricket. Nowhere near. Boxing was similar to cricket in that it was a case of, 'How much can I take?' But being punched in the face is more of a shock than a pain. You'll be sitting there after a spar or a fight, thinking, 'How did I get this black eye? I didn't even feel anything.' In contrast, playing cricket was often excruciating. I played 79 Test matches and people say to me, 'You must be gutted you didn't play more.' Not at all. I couldn't get out of bed some mornings.

In a weird way, I enjoyed hitting rock bottom more than I enjoyed being at the top. I didn't like the sliding part, but I relished the challenge of piecing myself back together again, getting back to where I wanted to be. In a sick way, I found it fun. I think that's why it happened quite a bit during my cricket career, maybe unconsciously on purpose, almost as if I was self-harming.

My cricket career was a mixture of massive highs and staggering lows, and my mind has fluctuated in much the same way. Maybe it needed to be that way. If everything had played out in monotone, I would have been bored. I love the bones off Alastair Cook, he's an amazing lad and an amazing cricketer, probably England's best-ever batsman, but the way he played, and continues to play, wasn't for me. I needed my cricket to be boom or bust.

I also wasn't good enough to play like Geoffrey Boycott, but I also enjoyed entertaining. What's the point of playing sport if you're not entertaining people? If Boycott was batting in my garden, I'd draw the curtains. Floyd Mayweather was the same in boxing. He was a genius, but he boxed not to get punched. I understand that, I've been punched and it's horrible. But I never got the sense that he loved what he did. He must have done, to keep going as long as he did, but he seemed far more interested in the lifestyle and the money than entertaining the fans. I could appreciate his greatness, but I would never have paid money to watch him fight.

I desperately wanted to win, but I also wanted to enjoy what I was doing, which meant I might be out first ball or score a hundred. That was part of the fun, neither me nor the crowd knowing what was going to happen. I enjoyed the adulation, the roar of the crowd when I hit a four or a six. That's one of the best sounds you can possibly hear, and I wish I could still hear it now. When the Barmy Army started chanting, I was going to have a crack. If they put a man back, I was going to try to hit it into the crowd. If a fast bowler pitched it up, I was going to try to hit it back over his head. I dug in a few times, when the state of the match decreed it, but I'd get bored and have to play a big shot, just to keep myself interested, never mind the punters.

Although the highs were brilliant, they were very short-lived. I'd come off the field after an England victory and think, 'Is that it? I'm already over this. What happens next?' Everyone harks on about what happened after the 2005 Ashes when we won them for the first time in almost 20 years – the open-top bus parade through London, the reception at Number 10, receiving an MBE from the Queen at Buckingham Palace. But I wasn't bothered about what happened afterwards – the celebrations, the adulation, the awards. The enjoyment came from doing it, and I reckon the reason I got so smashed afterwards was partly out of embarrassment. Even when people talk about that series now, I cringe inside. I don't want to still be dining out on it. Let it go, move on.

Every day of that series, I loved walking out there and doing battle with the Australians, and I wanted that feeling to last for ever. In between games, I went to Devon or France, so I didn't really know how big a stir the series was causing among the public. I did the odd interview, but once I'd done it, it just disappeared into the abyss. I never saw or read it, so it was like it never happened. It was only when it was over that it hit me how big a deal it had been. I'd just been playing cricket, but when that summer was over, everyone wanted a piece of me.

But I didn't want people telling me how good I'd been or slapping me on the back, and I wasn't buzzing and excited like my teammates. I just felt a bit guilty, almost as if I didn't deserve it. I'd done what I had to do and wanted to go home. That said, I wasn't happy that it was finished either. Why would I be?

I didn't fear hitting rock bottom in terms of form or fitness because I knew I could drag myself back up again. But I didn't even know I had depression. The cricket field was an awful place to be when I was playing badly, because it meant so much. But I could handle it, because my unhappiness was related to my form. The cricket field was safe. Even if things were going badly off the field – if my ex-girlfriend had sold a story to the *News of the World* or I was in trouble for being on the lash – I could not wait to play again. Cricket was what I did, what I knew, my whole identity. When I walked onto that field, you couldn't touch me, whether I was bowling to the best batter in the world and he was hitting me all over the park, or batting against the best bowler in the world and he was whistling the ball past my ears.

But there were times when I knew something was wrong with me, and I couldn't pinpoint what it was. This is one of the things people don't understand about depression. It's not like being unhappy when there's a reason. When you're a cricketer and you're unhappy with your form, you can fix it by hitting a century or taking five wickets. Depression is more like a numbness. At the 2007 World Cup in the Caribbean, I took a wicket against the West Indies and didn't even celebrate. When Chris Gayle hit my first ball for six, I thought, 'Ah well, that's modern cricket, the game has changed...' I went for tests, because I thought I might have a physical illness. Because I had no energy, I thought I might be diabetic or something, but the results came back all clear. Nobody suggested I might have a mental illness.

* * *

I'd been struggling with my knee for a long time before the 2009 Ashes series in England, so I had to decide whether to miss the series altogether and maybe give myself another two or three years in the sport, or play the six weeks. I decided to play, because I couldn't run away from being beaten 5–0 in the previous series Down Under. But during that series it got to the point where my missus was having to dress me in the morning. I couldn't move my leg, so I was trying to compensate by using other parts of my body, some of which I don't think I'd ever used. I was just so, so sore.

I somehow managed to play four of the five games in the series, but the writing was on the wall and I knew it was coming to an end. When you're playing, the games come so thick and fast that you take it all for granted. You stand in the field and you don't take things in or realise how lucky you are. It was only when I thought every day on a cricket field might be my last that I started to cherish every moment I was out there. I'd take in the ground, listen to the murmur of the crowd, look at the badge on my shirt, stare at my cap for ages. I felt like a child again, looking around and thinking, 'How good is this?' It's like that quote from golfing great Ben Hogan: 'As you walk down the fairway of life, you must smell the roses, for you only get to play one round.' I realised that too late in my cricket career, but at least I realised it.

When I took five wickets in the second Test at Lord's, I did that celebration where I fell to my knees with my arms outstretched. I'm a bit embarrassed about it, because it was completely self-indulgent. I regard myself as a team player, but on this occasion I didn't want any of my team around me. This was my last appearance at Lord's, the home of cricket. It was the best I'd ever bowled, given that my leg was about to fall off, I was jabbed up to the hilt and probably a little bit high. So it was all about me. I just wanted to smell the roses one last time and carry that smell with me for ever.

After the series was over, and we'd regained the Ashes, I had another micro-fracture operation, this time on my knee. I said to my surgeon, Andy Williams, a great fella from Bristol, 'I want to be awake, so you can tell me what's happening.'

He said, 'You do not want to be awake for this. My dad's a builder, I do the same job with different tools. I'm gonna get you in positions you do not want to see and make noises you do not want to hear.'

That swung it for me. The first part of the surgery involved tidying up my cartilage, but Andy warned me that if he found any bone damage, I was in trouble. He also told me that it was a 1-in-10,000 chance, but when I woke up, I looked at his face and said, 'I've got bone damage, haven't I?'

To which he replied, 'Yes.'

Whenever I'd done rehab before with Rooster, who practically lived with us, there had been light at the end of the tunnel. I'd rebuilt myself so many times that he probably got three or four years out of me I shouldn't have had. Whenever I'd been written off and told I couldn't do something, I'd told them to fuck off, through my actions at least. That was the worst thing you could possibly say to me, because whatever it was, I'd prove you wrong. I loved rebuilding myself that much. Even this time I gave it a go, despite the advice of my surgeon. But I soon had to admit I was beaten. In a hotel in Glasgow, over eggs Benedict, a specialist told me I was spent and would have to do something else. That was a bitter pill to swallow. It felt like I'd beaten myself. Having to retire was harder to take than any whitewash at the hands of Australia.

* * *

The BBC documentary about depression in sport was me and my management's idea. I wanted to do it because I had team-mates who'd struggled with it. Marcus Trescothick had returned home early from India in 2006, and later wrote with honesty and dignity about his mental illness. Steve Harmison had suffered for years in silence. I roomed with Harmy for years, spent days sitting on his bed watching *The Royle Family* or *Only Fools and Horses*. He even had every episode of *Lovejoy*, which I drew the line at. But I also saw him at his lowest, when he literally couldn't get off the floor. People just thought he was lazy, but the problem went far deeper. It was frustrating for me, because we were like brothers. I knew what he was going through, but I had to bite my tongue. So now I wanted to highlight what Harmy had been through, let him reveal his struggle, so that maybe it would make it easier for other people to speak about it.

This was about a year after I retired, when I was still wrestling with no longer being a cricketer, and the programme was almost like having therapy. I chatted to Ricky Hatton, who I love. Our careers hit the heights at the same time – just before the 2005 Ashes, he won the light-welterweight world title at the MEN Arena – and we used to bump into each other all over Manchester, drink to excess, sing karaoke together in the Press Club on Deansgate. And as I was listening to him speak, I was thinking, 'Hang on a minute, this is what I have. He's talking about me.'

And when I listened to Harmy speak I thought the same. I also listened to Celtic legend Neil Lennon – the same; former snooker world champion Graeme Dott, who spoke movingly about breaking down during a match and crying behind his hanky – the same. Everyone I spoke to, I could take pieces of their experiences and match them to mine. Making that programme was like a voyage of discovery.

I also went to America to interview Piers Morgan. He gave the press point of view, which wasn't necessarily his, and which sounded a bit harsh. But when they trailed the programme they took his quote out of context, so that it sounded like Piers was being insensitive. He wasn't, he was just explaining why the press are like they are, but he got hammered on social media. I felt a bit bad about that, because I like Piers and he'd done me a favour. While I was out there, he put me on to Vinnie Jones. I'd never met him, but when I phoned him up he said, 'All right, Freddie, course I know you, come over...' His place was on Mulholland Drive, which overlooks Hollywood. We went up there and were driving around, looking for his house, and suddenly we saw this great big Union Jack up a flag pole. We took a wild guess that it was Vinnie's gaff.

He was the perfect host, made brews for the crew as we were setting up in his kitchen. But when we did the interview, and he was telling me about the time he thought about shooting himself and his dog talked him out of it (it makes sense when you hear the full story), we had to keep stopping, because guests were arriving for a poker night and kept walking into shot.

Michael Greco was there, who played Beppe di Marco in *EastEnders*, 1980's football managers, American celebrities, and this lad called Keiran Lee, who's originally from Derby, is the highest-earning male porn star in America and owns a penis that is insured with Lloyd's of London for $1m. I had to say to Vinnie, 'Sorry, mate, can we stop these people walking through? We can't have porn stars wandering past, this is a documentary about depression.'

The night before, we'd watched David Beckham play football for LA Galaxy and ended up going out with him afterwards, because he was a friend of one of the lads in the crew. So Beckham phones up and invites us round for a bite to eat at his beach house in Malibu, which, it turns out, he's renting from Stephen Spielberg. So we're lounging about, his missus asks if we're hungry, and half an hour later we're in the cinema room – Stephen Spielberg's cinema room! – watching football and eating pizza. I should probably clarify: Beckham doesn't have depression (at least, it didn't look like he did) and we probably shouldn't have accepted his invitation. Just don't tell the BBC...

I think I've always had depression but didn't know it. I can identify behaviour as a child that could be seen as depressive. I isolated myself; things were never good enough. Now, when I come down with a bout, I feel like I'm surrounded by a grey fuzz. I can't engage in life. I want to get involved in a chat, but when I move my mouth nothing comes out. I can't even look people in the eye. I feel lethargic and nothing matters. I feel guilty, and guilty for feeling guilty. Rock bottom was not being able to get out of bed and just wanting to be asleep. The smallest thing might trigger it. Someone might say something, the shutters will come down and I'll sit in my pants watching *Storage Wars*, a programme about people bidding on the contents of a unpaid storage locker, for two weeks solid. That was a dark period in my life, my equivalent of Alan Partridge gorging on Toblerone and driving to Dundee in his bare feet.

But being told by a therapist that I was clinically depressed was a massive breakthrough and a huge relief. I remember filling in the questionnaire – 'Do you enjoy doing things as much as you used to? Do you lack energy and feel tired all the time? Do you not want to talk to people?' – handing it to this fella, him reading it and telling me I was depressed. I thought, 'No fucking shit! I could have told you that, it's why I've come to see you!' But at least now I categorically knew it was 'something', and that 'something' had a name. Before, I'd tried to self-medicate by drinking or eating too much. Now I knew what it was, I felt better equipped to deal with it.

Although I get depressed, it's not all doom and gloom. It's not the funniest of subjects, and it's difficult to normalise, because it's the strangest feeling. But I have to find some humour in it, otherwise it would do me in. There aren't many perks to having a mental illness. You can't get a blue badge and park closer to the door at Asda. Maybe they should have a look at that? Actually, it might cause problems. I was at Sports Direct recently, parked my car and had to walk miles. As I was walking in, this bloke pulled into a disabled spot, jumped out of his car, ran up to me and asked for a photo. I said to him, 'That's a bit out of order, mate, parking in a disabled spot, when you can run.'

This bloke looked at me in astonishment, pulled up his shirt and said, 'Mate, I've got a colostomy bag.'

'Oh. Shall we do this picture then...'

Imagine people trying to prove they're depressed? That might not end well. The only perk I can think of is that you can use it as an excuse for some questionable behaviour. Oh, and you're allowed to take a comfort dog on a flight. I reckon I must qualify. It's not even as if I've missed any work through mental illness, I've always been able to get out of bed, put on a face and plough on through it.

Another thing that amuses me about mental illness is the competitive element. You'll read the comments under an article about depression and there will be people talking about their experiences almost as if it's a sport: 'Oh, you're not as bad as me. When I get depressed it's ten times worse...' It's the same with recovering alcoholics. You'll speak to some of them and it will be like Top Trumps, or that Monty Python Four York-shireman sketch: 'I used to drink 15 pints every night and a bottle of whisky.'

'That's nothing. I used to drink 20 pints every night and two bottles of whisky.'

'You were lucky. I used to drink 50 pints every night, five bottles of whisky, three bottles of vodka, all from a rolled-up newspaper. And I got woken up every morning by having a load of rotting fish dumped all over me...'

It's not always plain-sailing, but I'm winning. I went through a few counsellors, because there's no point if you don't get on with them. I'm on medication, but that doesn't bother me. If I had a headache, I'd take an aspirin. If I cut myself, I'd put a plaster on it. It's not like the pills make me see unicorns and rainbows, they just make me feel normal.

I've upset mates because they thought I was being rude when, at the time, just making eye contact with someone felt like the hardest thing to do. There have been others who haven't been able to accept how I am. It's not that I don't like people, but I can be awkward to be around. It wasn't their fault. I didn't even know, so how were they supposed to?

Some people are able to put a face on, turn up to work and play the crowd before going home and curling up into a ball. I'd known Marcus Trescothick since I was 16. I'd toured with him all over the world and he was a good friend, but I didn't have a clue. People talk about team unity, but nobody knew about Marcus. Then, when he left the tour of India, he said he had a virus, because he didn't want anyone to know he had a mental illness.

A producer on *A League of Their Own* took his own life, and nobody had a clue he was struggling. You have a laugh and a crack with your mates and take the mickey out of each other, but you don't know how they're feeling or what they're going through. Not long ago, I was having a bout of depression and Robbie Savage noticed it. He kept sending me text messages. When you're feeling low, just a small thing like that can make a difference. Robbie is a very good mate.

Now I've got a better grip on it, I don't mind talking about it. That's not to say I wasn't worried about admitting it publicly. People had bought into this persona I'd built up over the years, and now I was telling them that it wasn't actually the real me. So when the documentary came out I was glued to Twitter, because I was so nervous about the reaction. I needn't have worried, because people thought it was brilliant. I had people coming up to me in the street and congratulating me, friends telling me that they had struggled as well. It was completely unexpected.

I hate the word 'stigma' when applied to mental illness. It's bandied around so much, but when people say, 'We need to overcome or break down the stigma', you're conceding there's a stigma in the first place. I don't think the stigma is anywhere near as great as it was, things have got so much better in recent years. I talked about injuries during my cricket career, and people talk openly about illnesses such as diabetes or cancer. Depression is no different.

If you're reading this and you have an inkling that something is not quite right, you don't enjoy things like they used to or you're having moods you can't explain, go to your doctor. When you're telling someone how you feel for the first time, you can feel the weight falling from your shoulders.

People hear sportspeople and actors and musicians talking about mental illness and think, 'What's he depressed about? He had a great career, he's rich, he's got everything.' But mental illness isn't selective, it can affect anyone, whether you're poor and anonymous or rich and famous. And famous people aren't coming out and talking about mental illness to get sympathy, they're speaking out to try to make a change. It's not easy to talk about it but sharing your story and experiences can have such a massive effect.

If I had been aware of it in my early teens, maybe life would have been easier. Then again, I've never wanted an easy life. If something is given to me, I've got very little interest in it. That's one of the biggest ironies of celebrity: the more famous and comfortable you become, the more people want to give you things for free. There are people sleeping on the streets with absolutely nothing, and companies are chucking clothes and bikes and all sorts at me. But only if you've earned something do you truly appreciate its worth. The things that are the hardest to achieve are the most rewarding. I've always wanted challenges, something to overcome. Depression is just another one of those challenges. It's horrible, and it can crush people, but it's made me who and what I am.

CHAPTER 8

WHY AM I HERE?

The mysteries of life

I love a conspiracy theory. I love watching programmes and reading books about them. Did the Moon landings happen? I'm undecided. Genuinely. I can't tell you either way, that's the thing about conspiracy theories, nobody really knows. I need hard and fast evidence. Show me, explain it to me. People say to me, 'They've got evidence, they've got film and photographs.' Have they heck. They could have been taken anywhere. Have you seen what they can do with cameras nowadays? What about the flag flickering, when there's supposed to be no atmosphere, and all that bouncing around? That filming was done in Nevada somewhere, in the middle of the desert.

They reckon they first went in 1969, but how the hell did they know they could get there? How did they know they could get back? Computers were so basic, and they were doing all the calculations on the back of envelopes with a pencil, compass and a ruler. And why have they not been back? People say it's because they've decided nothing's there. Really? People still go to Burnley and there's nowt there either. Other people say it's because it's too expensive, but they spend their money on loads of other rubbish, like Sheffield. You're telling me that nobody has thought, in the last 50 years, 'You know what, why don't we have another look? Maybe we missed something?'

Some people say the astronauts got warned off by aliens. There's a documentary called *Structures on the Moon*, which shows what look like buildings on the surface, so another theory is that Neil Armstrong, Buzz Aldrin and the rest of the lads got spooked. But I don't think they went in the first place. I wouldn't mind going to the Moon, and if I did, I think I'd be the first. Imagine having the Moon to yourself. I'd stay a couple of hours, float around a bit, do a couple of selfies, then come home again.

I listen to a programme called *The Flat Earth Podcast*, and they'll have you believing the Earth is flat and can't possibly be round. I'm not saying the world is flat – but it could be. Flat earthers say the Earth is like a disc, not completely flat, but bulbous underneath. While scientists believe the Sun is 149.6m km from the Earth, flat earthers believe it's only 4,000 miles above us, and the Sun and the Moon have the same dimensions, both with a diameter of 32 miles. The North Pole is in the middle of the Earth, and around the outside is the South

Pole, which is like a big wall of ice. This is why all governments now have got bases on the South Pole.

People say, 'But we've got photos and film of the Earth, taken from space, and it's quite clearly round.' But how do we know those pictures weren't doctored by NASA? If the world is round, why if you hover in a helicopter does your destination not come to you? Why, if we're hurtling through space, do lakes and seas stay relatively still? Why are they not wobbling all over the place? What about lasers? If the world was round, and therefore curved, if you fired a laser, why wouldn't it disappear at some point?

To be fair, I discussed this with Matthew Syed on our podcast, and he explained it in about 30 seconds. He said it was about the theory of relativity, something about travelling in an aeroplane and throwing a tennis ball in the air. That's the problem with educated people, they ruin everything. Even Robbie Savage thought I was being weird, which made me question myself, I have to admit. He was coming back with stuff about Aristotle seeing curved shadows on the Moon. And when Robbie tricked me into saying that the Earth might be shaped like a turnip, that's when I knew I might be on shaky ground.

One thing I don't understand about conspiracy theories is that, if there is any truth to them, there must be literally thousands of people in on them, and surely someone would blab. But what difference does it make if the Earth is round or flat? What does it matter? If it is actually round, why wouldn't the Flat Earth people say, 'You know what, we got it wrong, the world is round. But that's fine, let's all just have a cup of tea'? But you listen to them and they seem utterly convinced. When I brought this up on our podcast, everyone thought I was bonkers and a few of the papers wrote articles about me. Now, I'm not saying for one minute that the Earth is flat. Or round. It could be either. I've not been to space, so how can I say it is or it isn't with any degree of certainty?

There are 12 million people in the United States who believe that interstellar aliens in human suits are roaming the country. I'm not having that. I'm not going to go all David Icke on you and claim there are lizards walking about the place in human suits, just as I don't think I'm the son of God. But I do think there are aliens among us. Why wouldn't there be, when they reckon there are about 100 billion stars in our galaxy alone? I think it's more likely that there are aliens on Earth than aren't. I don't think they're like the aliens in *Men in Black*, blokes with ballbags hanging off their chins, or the fellas in *Star Wars*, with bums as faces. But for all we know, Burnley might be riddled with them. Half the staff at Greggs might be aliens. We just don't know.

And what about the pyramids in Egypt? There's no proper explanation for them, not even Egyptologists know how they were built. You're telling me they can't work out how the pyramids were built but they figured out a way to get to the Moon, 50 years ago? And there are pyramids all over the world – Africa, Central America, Asia, even a couple in the Antarctic. Man didn't build them, aliens did. Look at all the hieroglyphics and you'll notice the big boss in Egypt had a massive head. He's an alien. Then there are all these pictures of aliens with computers and spaceships. Some of the hieroglyphics depict lightbulbs and electricity, and this was 4,000 years ago, which fits in with another theory doing the rounds, that these aliens were so far advanced, right up until the point a meteorite hit them, when they had to start all over again.

There's also the conspiracy theory that time travel has already taken place. There's a photograph from the 1940s, from Canada, that shows a fella in a crowd of people wearing a printed T-shirt and wraparound sunglasses, surrounded by all these people who look like they should be from the period. It's not like it says 'Frankie Says Relax' on the T-shirt, but it's definitely a printed T-shirt. There's a painting from the 1930s that depicts a Native American scrolling through a smartphone in the 1600s. Apparently, there are theories in quantum physics that suggest it's possible to travel back in time, a bit like with *Back to the Future* and the flux capacitor.

I went through a period of lying on my back in the garden, staring at the sky and thinking, 'What is all this? I don't get it.' I sometimes think none of it exists. I'll be drinking a brew, thinking, 'Me, the tea I'm drinking, is this all just my reality? Or maybe I'm not really here?' It doesn't make any sense. Nothing makes sense in the world. I'll look at the kids doing their homework and think, 'Why have you spent all week learning about Henry VIII's wives? None of it matters, we're all wasting our time. And it's on the internet anyway.'

How can I be sat here, writing a book, knowing that there are people down the road living on the streets? How can it be that some people – including myself – sit around in luxury when other people have nothing? It's not that I'm happy that other people have nothing, it's just that I get on with my life without letting it affect me. How can it be that your dog gets fed twice a day and kids are dying because they haven't got anything to eat? I'll see someone walking along with a dog and think, 'How weird is that? Walking around with an animal on a string? Why are people so nice to dogs and not to other humans? Why do we teach them to shit outside? Why don't we just let them hang about with other dogs?'

Talking of dogs, I used to have two boxer puppies, and one day I was walking them down the river and let them off their leads. Off they went, bouncing down the path, and when I started shouting at them, they wouldn't come back. Suddenly, I realised they were chasing this little brown dog, who was barking its head off, before jumping into its owner's arms. When I arrived, my dogs were jumping all over this bloke, I was grabbing them by their collars, trying to pull them off, and I looked up and saw Roy Keane's very angry face looking back at me. I don't know if he recognised me, but I made my excuses and left sharpish. Maybe Roy was looking at me and my dogs and thinking, 'Is this all just *my* reality? Maybe I'm not really here?' Or maybe he was thinking, 'This bloke's a fucking idiot.'

I don't think anybody knows what's going on, it's like some massive free-form experiment. If you brought a Martian down and said, 'Mate, have a look at this place, what do you reckon?', they'd be completely baffled. Imagine if the Martian asked to be taken to your leader, because they wanted to see how things got done. You'd have to take them to the House of Commons and say, 'Right, that person over there is our prime minister, this lot over here, who are all shouting and screaming at each other, are going to ask her some questions, she'll do her best not to answer them, and once that's all wrapped up they'll all go home for tea.' You've got a fella in charge of the most powerful country in the world who loads of people think is a complete muppet and whose head looks like a Weetabix. The Martian would have a quick look around and request to be beamed back up again.

The pyramids or the Moon or the shape of the Earth are just the tip of the iceberg. If there is a universe, what's at the end of it? It can't just stop and then there's nothing. How did everything start? Scientists talk about a Big Bang, but from what? A single molecule? How big was this molecule? What was before the molecule? And what happens when it all ends? There has to be life after death, there can't just be nothing. There's no such thing as nothing, nothing doesn't exist, so when we die, it can't just go dark and that's it. And even if it does go dark, darkness is still something.

It bothers me, keeps me up at night. I'll be doing my hair in the mirror or deciding which shirt to put on, and suddenly I'll think, 'Why am I wasting my time with this? What happens when I'm dead?' It's the one thing you know is going to happen, but your average punter doesn't seem to give it any thought. Why would you not think about it? When is it going to happen? How is it going to happen? Will it be slow or quick, peaceful or painful?

People talk about feeling apprehensive before starting a new job, because they don't know what's going to happen. But they do know what's going to happen – they're going to put on a suit, sit behind a desk and tap on a computer. Of all the things people spend time thinking about, why is death not even on the list? Maybe when they're on their last legs they start thinking about it. But why not before? I'm told that most people get happier the older they get, which must be because they're relieved it's nearly all over.

You put the news on, hear the bongs of Big Ben, and they'll talk about all sorts – politics, war, famine, sport. But – and I'm not trying to play down the importance of discussing war and famine – why do they never talk about the big questions? The really important questions? Who cares if someone has been sacked from the Cabinet if we don't even know why we're here? Who cares if Man City won the Premier League if we don't know how it ends? People say it's pointless even talking about it, because there are no answers. But there have to be answers, and until I see the answers, I'll not rest.

I'll be in the queue at Poundland, see a couple of people wandering down the street and think, 'What are they doing? Where are they going at 3:30 on a Wednesday afternoon?' I'm not saying what I do is particularly remarkable, but what is anyone really doing? I'll see someone standing on a street corner and think, 'What's going through that person's head right now? Is he happy, sad, bored, fulfilled, lost?' I'll even do it with animals. I'll look at a dog and think, 'What's that dog thinking? Is he angry about being dragged about all day?'

People say it must be great, just lying on the floor in front of the telly. But dogs don't even know what's going on on the telly. Being a dog is basically ten years of doing nowt, being told what to do, reliant on someone feeding and watering you and letting you out of rooms. What's it like to be an ant? It's alive, it's got a head and a brain, but what does it do? What's it for? What about a frog? What does a frog do with its time, apart from croak? I know what a bee does, it flies around all day pollinating, but is it content? Is it happy conforming? We worry about Brexit, but what does a bee worry about? Does a bee want to be a wasp instead? Maybe being a wasp is a less pressurised job.

We experiment on rats and put insects in Petri dishes, and I sometimes wonder if someone is doing that with us, staring down a big microscope and saying, 'What are these dicks doing? What are they for? Are they happy? Why did they decide to be humans?' Who does decide to be born what they are? Why am I me and not that fella over there driving that van? Why am I not his dog? How does it all get divvied up? Is there a big meeting somewhere, with someone in the middle saying, 'Dogs over there, frogs over here'? There must be someone who decides what's what. I can't have it when people say, 'There is no designer, it's just science and nature.' There must be a designer! Science has got a lot to answer for. I think scientists make half of it up. Who's smart enough to challenge them, apart from other scientists? That's probably about 0.0001 per cent of the world's population. The rest of us have to take it on the chin.

Who designed science and nature? Who decides which sperm reaches the egg first? And after the sperm fertilises the egg, who decides what that egg turns out to be? Everything has to be designed. That car, this phone, that pen. It can't just be luck, that's a cop out. If it's luck, who designed luck? I sometimes fantasise about being given a choice. Someone says to me, 'You can spin this coin to decide whether you're going be the most successful person in the world, at whatever you choose to do, or a cockroach. Or, we can shake hands now and you'll be an orangutan.' I think I'd be an orangutan. Then again, we've cut all their trees down. Maybe I'd risk the spin.

The jury's out on reincarnation. I don't not believe in it, but I don't believe in it either. If everything is reincarnated, and we only started with a handful of people, how has it got to this? How has the population expanded like it has if it's on a one-for-one basis? And how do you know who's up for it? I'm not sure Buddha thought this through. I reckon that when I die, I'll come back with a good knee and play cricket again.

I met the Dalai Lama in South Africa. I was on the team bus in Durban and saw him leaving our hotel. I grabbed Andrew Strauss, talked my way past security, but when I got to the

Dalai Lama, I didn't know how to greet him. In the end I said, 'All right, Dal?' Straussy was mortified. The Dalai Lama just smiled and walked off.

I have my own religious beliefs, and while RE is the one subject I failed at GCSE, religion is the subject that's been of most use to me on my travels. When I toured Pakistan for the first time with England, I made sure I knew all about Islam, because I wanted to understand the place and its people. It was the same with Hinduism when I toured India and Buddhism when I toured Sri Lanka. I think religion is essentially about trying to be a better person. If you like a bit of what the Muslims do, use a bit of that. If you like a bit of what the Christians do, use a bit of that. There is no right or wrong way of doing religion, as long as you're being nice to people.

I don't go to church, because I don't believe that being religious means having to go to that building at the end of the road and worship with loads of other people. God is meant to be everywhere, isn't He? But I do try to remember to pray every night. I'm not a planned prayer, and I don't ask for stuff. I never dropped to my knees and asked God to allow me to get Sachin Tendulkar out the following morning. It's more that I want to thank God for what he's given me. It's also a form of therapy. It enables me to speak out loud and weed things from my mind, which can get quite overgrown at times.

If there is a God, who's God's God? Who's God's God's God's God? But I have to believe in God, because that's the only way I can make sense of anything. Either nothing is here, and all of this is complete nonsense, or God exists. Richard Dawkins argues against religion, but how can he argue when he doesn't know himself? Either this is a reality we created for ourselves, or there is a God who created it for us. Scientists have got theories, but we've all got theories. And my theory is that none of this exists.

I'm not sure if I believe in ghosts or not, but I'm scared of the dark. When we were kids, we'd wash the cars in the street, and as a reward, this fella Barry would let us watch movies in his front room. We started off with *Rocky* and *Raiders of the Lost Ark*, before graduating to *The Exorcist*. I was only nine. It triggered nightmares and meant I ended up on pills and all sorts.

When I walk into a dark room, I get butterflies ten times worse than when I walked out to bat. I have to leave the landing light on at night. I say it's for the kids. I think I might have seen a ghost a few years ago. Then again, I was half asleep, and the light was off. If I was a ghost, I'd pop up and show myself to people when they were in the supermarket or having a cup of tea in the garden. But why do we not put serious effort into finding out if they exist or not? It's quite a big thing, is it not? Instead, we've got Yvette Fielding on the telly, stumbling around old houses in the dark with no torch.

Which reminds me, when I was a kid I had a pet tortoise I thought died and came back to life. This tortoise was called Fred. (I'm a bit of a one-trick pony when it comes to names – I had a dog called Fred, a teddy called Fred. If I had a pony I'd probably call it Fred.) When Fred passed away, my mum said she'd bury him while I was at school. She left him on the top of the bin, the binmen came, saw this tortoise and put him back in the garden. God knows how they thought he got on top of the bin. When I got home from school, I was running around the place shouting, 'It's a miracle! Mum, he's come back to life!' I played with dead Fred for a week, because my mum didn't have the heart to tell me that he hadn't actually been resurrected like some tortoise Jesus.

How often do you sit around and discuss these questions, which are some of the biggest in the world? I suppose it would end up driving us all mad. That's probably why I am mad, because I think about it too much. When you sit down to get your hair cut and the barber starts asking you where you're going on your holidays, why don't you say, 'Don't patronise me, ask me how the world started. Or what happens when we die. Or whether aliens exist. Or who's God's God's God'? But if you did bring it up in the barber's, or down the pub, people would roll their eyes, sigh and say, 'Bit heavy, innit?'

But I don't find it heavy, I find it strangely liberating. I wish I'd felt a bit more this way when I was younger, it would have given me so much more freedom. I look back at some of the things that used to bother me and think, 'Why?' I was pissed trying to get on a pedalo in the Caribbean – so what? Who really cares? It doesn't matter in the grand scheme of things. If I don't know how the world started or whether any of this is actually real, why would I be bothered about hitting a ball with a bat? I'm going to die, I don't know whether any of this is real or not, but I'm terrified of being bowled by Zaheer Khan, last over before close of play at Trent Bridge? It's all complete madness.

CHAPTER 9

NOT CURING CANCER

Just doing a job

I played in Soccer Aid at Old Trafford and was very grateful to be asked. But if I could raise money for Unicef by having a kickaround in the garden with my mates, I'd do that instead. There was nothing wrong with anyone, but I tend to retreat in those kinds of situations. I don't just hate small talk, I detest it. I'm quite comfortable in silence. People sometimes think I'm rude, but I'll be standing there thinking of something to say and won't be able to. A barman will make a quip and I won't know what to reply with. I'll be walking down the street, someone will walk past and make a comment, and I'll be dumbstruck. If someone makes a wisecrack in the street or the supermarket, my natural instinct is to tell them to piss off, but I bite my tongue and say nothing instead.

While I was working for *The Project*, they were trailing the first Australian series of *I'm a Celebrity… Get Me Out of Here!* There was the usual guessing game as to who was going in, and when it came out that there was a cricketer involved, people started saying it was me, which it wasn't.

I had no interest in sitting around in a jungle for a few weeks with a load of people I didn't know, just to be on the telly. I'd been asked to do the British version loads of times and always said no. And when I got home from Melbourne, and was settling back into my life in England, I got a call from the makers of Australian *I'm a Celeb*, asking if I'd enter the jungle late. I said no again, but they kept on upping the offer, until after two or three offers things were getting interesting. I started thinking, 'It's only a month, and all I've got to do is sit about and chat nonsense.' In the end, they made me an offer I couldn't refuse. I was on *The Jonathan Ross Show* and when I came offstage, my wife was sitting in the green room with my agent. She said, 'You're off to the jungle on Friday…' So straight from interviewing Will Smith and Margot Robbie in LA, I flew back to Australia and entered the jungle.

The fact I hate making small talk is one reason I don't really thrive in a celebrity environment. God only knows how I won *I'm a Celeb*. I'm told it's because I wasn't trying to be anyone else but me. And once you start dabbling in celebrity circles, you realise there are an awful lot of people who try to be anyone else but themselves. It was the easiest month of my life, I just sat there losing weight and getting paid. My contract said I couldn't get booted out before two weeks were up, so I slept for a fortnight before upping my game. I was sat there thinking, 'If I make it through the weekend, maybe we can get a new patio?'

I get fed up of people wittering, talking about nothing. People they've never met, people on *Love Island*, someone they read about in *Grazia* magazine. I'll be standing there thinking, 'I don't want to be involved in this conversation, I don't know how to be involved in this conversation, I want to be euthanised right now, while this conversation is going on.' People will watch a programme about people pretending to live in a street in Salford and then try to tell me all about it. What is it about their own lives that they've got to watch other people's pretend lives, which are really quite depressing? I can't really talk, I used to watch *Corrie* all the time.

I don't get why people feel the need to shout things at me when I'm out. I was out filming in Manchester recently, with a cardboard cut-out of some bloke, and someone shouted, 'Take your finger out of his arse!' I thought about saying something back but could only think of bad things and that might have caused a problem for my crew. People will see me and scream,

'Where's your pedalo?' It happened 11 years ago, but they'll act as if they're the first person who's ever said it. People will shout 'Jacamo!' at me, because I'm on their adverts. How are you supposed to react to that? And if I don't turn around they sometimes get offended.

I don't mind people asking me for an autograph or a selfie, there's nothing wrong with that. But other people will come up to me and say, 'Are you who I think you are?' I'll say, 'I don't know, who do you think I am? Denzel Washington?' Other people will come up close, stand there staring and say to their mate, 'Do you know who that is?' These are grown adults! What kind of weird world do they live in where that's acceptable behaviour? Even stranger than that, people will say, 'I don't know who you are', and stand there gawping at me. If you don't know who I am, why are you bothering me? I think them telling me they don't know who I am is their little victory, another way of saying, 'I know you must be famous, because I've seen those other people ask for a picture, but you're not as famous as you think, because I've never heard of you.' Other people will tell me they don't like something I've done on the telly or someone I've worked with who's a mate of mine. It's just really difficult to get your head around.

When I was in Ireland, filming with the chip van for *Lord of the Fries*, I was in bed in my hotel room, at about 1 a.m., and I heard giggling outside my room. Then I heard the door handle being jiggled. I thought, 'It'll be all right, they can't get in.' But then I heard a key card being slid in and the door opening. A girl's head popped around the wall and she said, 'Could I have a photograph?' I was thinking, 'I can't get out of bed, because I'm naked, and all of a sudden I'd be the wrong 'un.' After some gentle but persistent persuasion, she left.

The following morning, I went down to complain to the manager. 'Look, mate, someone got in my room last night and I don't even know who it was.'

'Oh...'

'What do you mean, "Oh..."?'

'That'll be the ghost...'

I don't know much about ghost etiquette, but I'm almost certain they don't need a key card or ask for selfies.

After stints overseas and down south, I'm now back up North, living in a leafy town in Cheshire. The locals are very good to me, I can pop to the shops or the gym and the most I'll get is a cheery 'All right, Fred', which is lovely. I love shopping in Poundland, because I get a proper buzz from finding things cheap, and I eat in Nando's, wander around the markets and travel on the tram. Occasionally, I'll find myself in situations where I'm out with the wife and kids and I'll have to say, 'Look, I've got to look after my family here', and if it gets too much I'll just make a quick exit. But my kids have grown up around it and people are generally respectful.

Since I gave up booze a few years ago, I don't really go anywhere or do anything on my own, I'd rather just stay at home with the family. I don't thrive in big groups and get a bit anxious with a lot of attention. I don't mind the attention that comes with doing something, like on the cricket pitch or the stage, because nobody can get to you. But when people can get to me, I get in a bit of a flap. That's why I disappeared after the 2005 Ashes, and maybe why I got so smashed during the bus parade, because I didn't like being so exposed.

Adulation is a very strange thing. I've always thought that the treat was playing, not the slaps on the back and the awards and medals. Along with the rest of the 2005 Ashes-winning team, I won an MBE. But cricket was my job, just something I did. Actually, I didn't even see it as a job, because it was something I loved doing so much. Why would anyone want to give you an MBE for living your dream? Just walking out to bat for England was enough.

People talk about the sacrifices sportspeople make to get where they've got, but if making all those sacrifices is such a chore, do something else. It's not like you're grafting down a mine every day, or looking after the elderly or disabled, you're just going running or cycling or lifting weights in the gym.

Every time I visit Old Trafford, I feel proud. I'll walk around, see all the pictures and bats and jumpers on the walls, and I'll feel part of something special. When I was 20, Lancashire were paying me £40 grand a year. I went into a contract meeting and told them that Sussex and Hampshire had offered me £110 and £120 grand a year respectively. They said, 'So go then.' But I didn't want to play for Sussex or Hampshire. In the end, they upped the offer to £60 grand, which was still half what I could have got elsewhere, and when they called me in to sign the contract, it said £55 grand on it. I signed it anyway, because Lancashire was the only team I ever wanted to play for.

But I don't even know where most of my England caps and jumpers are. Mum's got a few, and the boys love the Sports Personality of the Year and World Player of the Year trophies. But I didn't play for them; winning awards was never my ambition. All I wanted to do was win trophies for Lancashire and the Ashes for England. That was enough.

I see people I work with begging for votes on social media, for this or that programme, and it baffles me. When we won a Bafta for *A League of their Own*, I stayed at home, watched *Game of Thrones* and found out on Twitter. We won three Aria awards for the podcast, but I already knew we were doing a decent job, because I could see the listening figures and download numbers. I could see it meant a lot to Robbie, which is why I went along with him to the ceremony, but I couldn't have cared less. Don't get me wrong, I wanted to win, because I really enjoy doing the podcast and am proud of what we do. But having to go up onstage and receive the awards was just embarrassing. Maybe if I won an Oscar or a Bafta for acting I'd think differently. Can you imagine me crying like Gwyneth Paltrow? I think the speech would go something like, 'I don't do it for the awards and adulation, I do it for the people...'

Awards are subjective, and I don't like anything that's subjective. I like black and white, win or lose. People's opinions of what I've done isn't important to me, apart from maybe my mum's. Being on TV and doing fun things is the privilege, because they're things people would cut their arms off to do. That's why I feel like I have a responsibility to enjoy what I do. I struggle sometimes, because it's never what I set out to be. I'll do a show and everyone will be buzzing, but I'll be thinking, 'I just want to go home now.' There's even a part of me that feels like I don't deserve it. But I do enjoy it, in my own way. And that should be why you do anything, not because you might win an award at the end of it.

I've heard celebrities having these deep discussions about who should be knighted, or given this award or that medal, and I just think, 'These shouldn't be going to people who act or sing or cycle around France every summer, these should be going to people who make a real difference', like doctors and nurses in A&E or people grafting in laboratories trying to find the cure for cancer. The people who clean our sewers or collect our rubbish are more valuable to society than a bloke who runs around for a living.

My dad was a plumber by trade and then worked for British Aerospace on a machine. It was proper work, and that's why I didn't ask them to come to Buckingham Palace when I got my MBE. They would have loved it, and the fact I didn't is one of the few genuine regrets I have in life. I had three tickets, but ended up just taking my missus. I found it all a bit embarrassing.

Only six weeks after regaining the Ashes, we'd lost a Test series in Pakistan. We got found out, because we weren't working hard enough. I'd turned up a stone overweight, and I wasn't the only one. Factions had started appearing in the dressing room, you could just tell things weren't right.

When it really hit me was after the final Test in Lahore. All the lads who played in the Ashes series were summoned to the team room and in walked the high commissioner, who said, 'I've got some good news, Her Majesty has bestowed awards upon you in her New Year's Honours.' This fella went around the room, reading our names and full addresses out, asking us if we wanted to accept, and obviously we all said yes. But I couldn't help thinking, 'This is all well and good, but we've just had our pants pulled down.'

The whole thing just felt absurd, especially because I didn't think I should have been getting an award at all. Duncan Fletcher, the coach, got an OBE. Come on! He just picked the team! The skipper, Michael Vaughan, got an OBE as well, for moving the fielders around. Paul Collingwood got an MBE for scoring 17 runs in the final Test. Was he embarrassed? Bollocks was he! He was the first to accept it. Seventeen runs and he was cracking the champagne open. If I was him, I would have rejected it as a matter of principle. Instead of joining in, I left them to it. It was then that I realised that the team had real problems.

I'd love to be honoured by my country again, somewhere down the line, but for something more important than just hitting a ball. When I'm old and sitting in front of the fire with a rug over my legs, I'd like to be able to look at a medal I was given and think, 'You know what, I'm really proud of what I did to get that.' But I don't even know where my MBE is. I know my mum gave it to my Auntie Joan for a bit, God bless her. Auntie Joan looked like Richie Benaud, but she was a great woman and used to spoil me and my cousins rotten. After she started losing her memory, I went round to visit her in her little bungalow and she was sat there in her chair with my MBE on her chest. I said to her, 'What you got on?' She said, 'It's my MBE. Have you got one?'

CHAPTER 10

HARD, FAST AND SHORT OF A LENGTH

A fine romance

I'm not a romantic. I try to be, but I'm not very good at it. Whenever I try to be romantic, things backfire. I'm from Preston, we don't really do romance up here. In fact, I don't really know what is romance and what is just stupid. There are certain subjects I'm good at, and other subjects where I'm firmly in the bottom set. As far as romance is concerned, I'm the kid at the back of the class eating worms and wearing a dunce's hat.

You've got to remember that as a kid growing up, I was a cricketer. Try to woo a girl by telling them you play cricket and she won't show a flicker of interest. It's nothing like telling them you're a professional footballer or rugby player. Oh, and I also played chess. I found that most girls found boys who were into football sexy, as well as boys who took drugs and boys who beat people up. I wasn't into any of that. Girls found cricketers about as sexy as chlamydia.

Suffice to say I didn't have much of a romantic grounding as a teenager. As a kid, I was useless, shy and virtually mute. I always liked girls but didn't know what to do. I'm surprised I ever lost my virginity. When I played my first second team game for Lancashire, I was in the dressing room and Joanna Lumley came on the telly. She was advertising yoghurt, and at one point she licked the lid. The coach said, 'Would you?' I thought he was talking about licking yoghurt off the lid, so I replied, 'I wouldn't just lick it off the lid, I'd lick it straight from the pot.' My first trip away with the second team, the lads set me up with this woman in a nightclub. At one point I thought I'd moved to second base, so to speak, and when I looked down I had my finger in a bottle of Hooch. That's how naive I was.

The lads used to send me into the petrol garage to buy porn mags. I'd walk in, wearing my full Lancashire tracksuit, and walk out with about 20 of them. The people behind the counter must have thought I was a proper wrong 'un. When I got back to the team bus, all the lads would be on tenterhooks: 'Have you got 'em? Did you remember to get *Razzle*?' Nowadays, kids can find everything out on the internet. There are online courses that teach you to play the piano in 20 days, but kids can be experts in sex in less than that. Magazines were all well and good, but they didn't show you what to do. That said, I'm not sure the modern idea of what sex is supposed to be like is healthy. For a start, you don't normally have someone watching in the real world. And it's not every day you do it in the street or on top of a car. These aren't prerequisites for sex, but I have a horrible feeling some kids think they are.

I lost my virginity when I was 17. I was out with some lads in the Phoenix nightclub in Manchester, got talking to this Indian medical student and, before I knew it, I was kissing her outside the fire exit. She was 23, I told her I was 19. We went back to her place, fell into her bedroom and everything started going wrong. I had a condom on me, but I couldn't get it on. I was trying to pull it on like a sock. In a state of blind panic, I staggered out into the hallway, was leaning against the wall, trying to compose myself, when the front door opened and her brother walked in. I bade him a cheery hello before falling back into the bedroom and resuming operations. After some very amateurish fumbling on my part, she said, 'Have you done this before?' I replied, 'Oh yeah, I've done it a few times, don't you worry about that...' Technically, I don't think I lost my virginity that night, because no part of it was anywhere near where it was supposed to be. Not much different to my Test debut. I'm no good at debuts full stop. I take a while to get my eye in.

I had my 40th birthday party at the Ocean Beach club in Ibiza. Everywhere you looked there were women in bikinis and if it had been my 21st birthday party, it would have been the best place ever. But I couldn't help thinking, 'All these girls are some blokes' daughters.' If my daughter was wandering around a nightclub in a bikini, it would kill me. I was in Scotland, filming the fish and chip programme, and one of the young kids from production was in the van with me. He saw this girl walk past in a very short skirt and his tongue was hanging out of his head. My first thought was, 'I bet she's got cold legs...'

*   *   *

When I first started going out with Rachael, I came in one night at about 3:30 a.m. and handed her a kebab. She was over the moon. It wasn't really the kebab that made her happy, it was the fact that I was thinking of her. We sat and ate our kebabs together in bed, and it was a beautiful moment. But the course of love hasn't always run so smoothly.

Before I met Rachael, I'd been seeing this other girl for years. Christmas Eve 2001, I returned from a Test series in India and it had been planned that we'd do our Christmas shopping and spend Christmas Day at my mum and dad's. But when I arrived at Manchester airport, nobody had turned up to collect me. When I phoned my girlfriend, she wouldn't answer. Eventually I jumped in a cab and when I got home my girlfriend was waiting for me, but to say the reception was a bit frosty is an understatement. I went shopping on my own and bought her a diamond bracelet, but when I gave it to her on Christmas morning, along with her other presents, I got nothing back. So I went to my mum and dad's on my own.

I had no contact with her for about a fortnight, and when I came back, I opened the door and it was like I'd been burgled. Almost everything had gone, the place was like a shell. I went upstairs and the bacon butty and cup of tea I'd made her on Christmas morning were still there, going mouldy, as was her Christmas card. Funnily enough, the diamond bracelet was gone.

I had to go back to India the following day for a one-day series, and for the first couple of weeks I was quite down about the whole situation. Then I started to think, 'This is an opportunity more than anything.' I started going to the gym, got fit and put myself back on the market. The cricket was going well, off the field was going well, and when we moved on to New Zealand, things got even better.

In Hamilton, I got a message under the door of my hotel room, from the local police. It said: 'Ring your fiancée.' I phoned her and she said, 'Andrew, I made a mistake...' So I replied, 'Yes, I think you have. I'm on tour with England, I've got myself in shape and I'm having an absolute ball...'

Problem was, I got done by the *News of the World* for going out with a couple of girls while I was in New Zealand. I'd had plenty of stories written about me before that were complete bollocks, but this one was absolutely spot-on. The reporter had obviously been following me all night. He knew what we'd eaten, what wine we'd drunk, that we'd ended up in a jacuzzi on the roof of the hotel. Now my ex has really got the hump, so when I finally get home, I discover she's emptied our joint account, so that I'm pretty much skint. On top of that, she's sold her story to the *News of the World* and the journalist who wrote it has phoned my parents for a comment.

On the Saturday of the second Test of the summer against Sri Lanka in Birmingham, I met Rachael. I saw her in the executive box and thought, 'She's nice, I'd love to talk to her.' I got her number, sent her a text and signed off with 'Fred'. She replied with, 'Who's Fred?' I had to explain that I was the chubby England cricketer with a skinhead. I met her in the bar after the day's play, it went well, so I asked if she fancied a bite to eat on Sunday evening because it looked like the match was going to finish early. Luckily, she said yes.

On the Sunday morning, I was walking towards the dressing room and I could hear people sniggering and whispering, 'He's here! He's here!' When I went in, everyone was sitting there reading the *News of the World*. I asked them what they were reading, and somebody said, 'It's about you!' They gleefully showed me the article and the headline read: 'FLINTOFF'S LOVEMAKING LIKE HIS BOWLING – HARD, FAST AND SHORT OF LENGTH'. I'm told the actual story was far worse.

I had to go out and field and bowl, and the skipper Michael Vaughan put me out in front of the bouncy stand, so that I was getting hammered all day by the crowd. When Ashley Giles took the final wicket to wrap up the win, I was the most relieved man in Birmingham. That night, I asked Rachael if she'd read any press about me recently, and she said she'd read a lovely piece about me in *The Times*. A few drinks later, she admitted she'd seen the story about me in the *News of the World*. She didn't mind, we had a laugh about it, but the article left a lingering scar that would come bursting open later that summer.

Because Rachael worked for Npower, who were sponsoring the cricket, we started seeing more and more of each other, and when we played in Manchester, she was going to stay with me, to take the relationship to another level, so to speak. But because I was worried about living up to my reputation, as laid out in the *News of the World*, I phoned my old mate Paddy in Liverpool and asked if he could get hold of a few Viagra tablets. He got me three of them.

The plan was that Rachael was going to meet some friends on the Saturday, have a few drinks, then come back and meet me at the Marriott. So when we finished that day's play, I was right on the edge. I had a pint in the dressing room, went back to the hotel, had another pint with the lads, retired to my room, popped a Viagra, watched *Coronation Street* and had another couple of pints. At nine o'clock, Rachael still hadn't turned up, so I popped another Viagra. It got to eleven o'clock and she still hadn't turned up, so I thought, 'Fuck it, I'll pop another one, just to counteract the booze.' Half an hour later, every part of me was stiff. I was sweating, in a right pickle, so when she finally rocked up at about one in the morning, I told her I had a headache.

When I woke up the next morning, I was still stiff all over, and the bloody thing wouldn't go down. I'm driving to the ground, listening to Steve Wright's Love Songs, and it just refuses to crumple. And when I arrive at the ground, it's still standing to attention. I'm in the dressing room, trying to put my whites on and having to hold it to one side. I go out for warm-ups with a hand in my pocket, and when someone asks if I want to have a bat, I have to hold the bat with my top hand and stuff my other hand down my trousers.

I'm batting six, so when we lose a couple of wickets, I think I'd better go and put my kit on. But I can't put my box on properly, so have to balance it on top. We lose another couple of wickets, and it's my turn to bat. In a panic, I tuck it into the waistband of my undies and leave the box off. I get announced on the tannoy – 'Next in, Lancashire's own Andrew Flintoff!' – the crowd goes up and I'm walking out like a penguin. A minute later, I'm standing at the crease, this fast bowler Fernando, who's really quite rapid, is running towards me, and I'm thinking, 'I've not got a box on, I've got a full-blown erection and I'm playing for England on my home ground. What on earth is going on here?'

I manage to score one run before Alec Stewart hits it back towards me, I'm out of my ground, and the ball flicks the bowler's hand. So now I've got a split-second decision to make: if the ball hits the stumps, I'm out. But if I make a dive for it, I might snap my old fella in half. Worse, it might fall out. So I just stand there instead, and am run out by a mile. When I get back to the dressing room, Duncan Fletcher, the coach, is seething. He says to me, 'What the hell was that?' I reply, 'I'm a bit stiff, Duncan...' At least I told the truth.

While I was sitting in the dressing room, contemplating yet another ridiculous situation in my life, it finally subsided.

But because I was waiting on a hernia operation, I had to have treatment every day. So Dean Conway, this 19-stone Welsh physio, is working on my groin and it suddenly goes up again, like an inflatable toy. So I say, 'Dean, it's not you. Let me tell you a story...'

CHAPTER 11

NUMBER TWO IN A BAG

The daft things I've done

Then there was the time I pooed my pants at Lord's. Me and Darren Gough, being a bit on the chubby side, were always trying to lose weight, any way we could. So when these Xenical pills came on the market, we both got stuck in, like they were Smarties. When you take one of these pills, it separates the fat from the food, which is horrible when it comes out. It's supposed to encourage you to eat better, but me and Goughie thought popping a few Xenical meant we could eat whatever we wanted.

There was one major problem with Xenical – when you had wind and trumped, you were in serious trouble. So I was sat there in the dressing room at Lord's, I farted and it all came tumbling out. The boys are already out in the middle, and I'm next into bat. So I'm thinking, 'If either of them gets out, what do I do? I've just cacked my pants. I can't go out like this at Lord's, the home of cricket. What would WG Grace say?'

In the corner of the dressing room is a sink, so I whip everything off, sit in the sink and wash myself, while I'm trying to watch the game through the window, in case anyone gets out. Nasser Hussain, the skipper, is looking at me like I've just crawled out from under the skirting board. Goughie is rolling about on the floor laughing. Luckily, I'm pulling my pants back up just as it's my turn to go out and bat. Even more luckily, I score a few runs. I think Nasser saw the funny side eventually.

I first played for Lancashire's second team when I was only 15. I'd played for Lancashire Under-15s the day before, and this old boy called John Savage, who was a scout, asked if I was available. I told him to speak to my dad, my dad said yes, and the following morning I turned up at Old Trafford for a three-day game against Glamorgan with a load of professional cricketers.

I just wanted to play cricket, and when I had a bat or ball in my hands, I probably seemed quite manly. But I was really quiet and innocent in many ways, there was nothing worldly about me. I walked in the dressing room and some of the lads were all right, but some of them seemed a bit put out that this spotty teenager was in their team.

I didn't have a helmet, so I walked out to bat in an England Schools cap, which one of their fast bowlers tried to knock off. I scored 20-odd, got overconfident, tried to smack one over the top and got caught. Not bad for a 15-year-old, but the chat in the dressing room – about booze and birds and sex – was a complete mystery. But at the end of the game, someone handed me an envelope, I opened it and there was 60 quid inside. I thought, 'I get paid to play cricket?' As soon as I'd done my GCSEs, I dropped everything else, because all I wanted to be was a cricketer.

A few weeks later, I had my first trip away with the second team, down in London. I sat at the front, in my shirt, tie and blazer, and all the old pros piled down the back with this big cooler full of beer. Before we'd reached Stoke, I was six cans in and had my tie wrapped around my head. All three days got rained off, and back then you didn't do anything if play was abandoned. So I spent my time in the bookies, betting on dogs and horses with my meal money, before heading to a nightclub with the rest of the team. When I got home, I had to speak in assembly about my experiences. Obviously, I lied through my arse. I'm not sure the teachers would have appreciated stories about fingering a bottle of Hooch in a nightclub.

My second game was against Kent, and I batted against Richard Ellison, who had played about 400 games for his county and 11 Tests for England. He had this big eighties' tache, big permed hair, and was still angry, despite being more than twice my age. First ball he teed right up, I smacked him for four through the covers and he came down the pitch and started chuntering at me. Second ball, exactly the same thing. I was thinking, 'Tee it up again, and I'll smack you again. What else am I supposed to do?' And that's what happened.

I just wanted to be accepted, but it was an intimidating environment for a 15-year-old. Grown men were coating me because I was a virgin and had no pubes. I wouldn't have a shower, because I was embarrassed. People thought it would be funny to show me up in front of women. They'd call them over, introduce me and I'd be going bright red and sweating. It toughened me up, but none of that would be allowed now, quite rightly. I wouldn't want my boys to see and hear some of the stuff I saw and heard in the dressing room.

When I started playing for the first team, I got my head down and didn't really speak. That all changed on an end-of-season trip to Guernsey, when I was 17 or 18. I scored a hundred, which I thought was a big deal, but it was really just a lash-up. Afterwards, my teammates started playing drinking games with Guinness. I started out with Coke but got sick of it after a few glasses and switched to the black stuff, like the other lads. It turned out I was good at drinking. I had ten pints that night and suddenly I was one of the gang.

Being part of the gang meant being party to the dressing-room banter. When I first started playing for Lancashire's second team, it was full of average players, lads in their late teens and early 20s who thought they were on the verge of making it but who were never going to be cricketers. They loved the lifestyle, drinking every night after playing, swanning around in their Lancashire kit. And all that bravado made the dressing room a horrible place at times. If anyone had a fault, however minor, people would jump all over it. And if someone jumped all over you, you had to jump all over them, to show you had something about you.

It was a tough school, nasty at times. I remember me and my best mate Paddy playing for the Under-19s against the second team, and when we went out to bat, they started abusing us. I was a pro at the time, supposedly one of them. Paddy's a Scouser, a proper hard bloke, so he turned around to me and said, 'Are we gonna have this or not?' I replied, 'Yeah, whatever you do, I'll go with you.' We didn't take a backward step, hit them all over the park, and Paddy would deliberately hit the bowlers with his bat as he ran past. Me and Paddy were kindred spirits, looked after each other. In that kind of environment, you needed people in the dressing room who had your back.

Then again, you couldn't even trust your best mates. I played one game for the second team, scored 30-odd, got out and was livid with myself. Rather than going straight to the dressing room, I went to the toilets, to have some time with myself and calm down a bit. I was sat in a cubicle, with my back to the door and my feet on the toilet, contemplating life, and once the anger had subsided, other things started entering my mind. I started playing a bit of absent-minded 'pocket billiards', and you know what it's like when you're young, things just happen that you hadn't really planned.

Suddenly, I had the sense that someone was watching me, before I saw Paddy's head under the door and heard his thick Scouse accent: 'All right there, Freddie lad?' He went back to the dressing room, told everyone what he'd seen, and when I walked in they were all on the floor laughing. I was only 17, so didn't know where to put myself. Even worse, Paddy told that story at my wedding. We'd just finished the profiteroles and Paddy got up and started saying, 'Ladies and gentlemen, you know how some people get angry when they get out at cricket? Well, Freddie gets aroused...' I could hear my nan talking to my auntie: 'What did he say, Barbara? Something about billiards?'

The dressing room is one of the places you miss most when you retire, it's where adults can act like kids for eight hours a day. A lot of what went on was simply down to boredom. We had so much time to fill, we had to do something. So instead of studying for degrees, we'd get a bottle of Tabasco out and see how much we could drink. Another time, I drank 12 cans of Red Bull, just to see what it would do to me. But some of what went on in the dressing room was plain bullying, with no redeeming features. It had nothing to do with team bonding, it just made the person who was doing the bullying feel a bit better, and I found it was worse from the lesser players in the team.

One day, I was playing at Middleton Cricket Club, was in the shower after close of play and could feel something warm running down my leg. Darren Shadford, who is one of the thickest people I have ever met, was pissing on me, laughing like an idiot. I just looked at him and said, 'Don't worry, Darren, I will get you back.' And if I get it into my head that I'm going to do something, I will do it, whether it's singing in a musical or gaining revenge on someone who's pissed down my leg in the shower.

A few months later, Darren walked out to bat on this baking hot day, I went into his locker, nicked his car keys, found a carrier bag, did a dump in it and tipped it into the passenger-door pocket of his brand-new, sponsored Rover 214.

I didn't tell anyone what I'd done, returned the keys to his locker and hung around in the car park after play had finished. As he was driving off, with all his windows wound down, I could hear him shouting, 'Fuckin' 'ell! It stinks in this car! Stinks!'

The next day, Darren walked into the dressing room and was livid: 'Who did that in me car? Who was that?' Everyone else was looking at each other, but I had my head between my knees. Someone asked him what had happened, and he replied, in this wheezy Oldham accent, 'Well, when I left Old Trafford, I went to pick the missus up from work. She got in the passenger seat, put her hand in the door pocket, where she keeps the humbugs, and pulled out a turd. Whoever did that is fuckin' disgusting.' At that point I decided to own it. I said, 'Darren, I did tell you I'd get you back for pissing on me. I think we're equal now...' He erupted, but I said to him, 'Mate, it's up to you how we take it from here, but I suggest we just leave it.' And he did.

Glen Chapple, my old Lancashire captain, was nicknamed the 'Ginger Pig', which he wasn't a big fan of. Before the Open Championship at Birkdale in 2008, I went to this barbeque at Ernie Els' house, because we had the same agent. He had this hog roast, and I persuaded the chef to give me the head. I got a taxi back to Altrincham, with this pig's head in a carrier bag, got the cabbie to swing by Old Trafford, told the bloke on the gate I'd left something in the dressing room, broke into Glen's locker and put this pig's head in there, with his Lancashire cap on top. The following day, I went off with England. What I'd forgotten was that the Lancashire lads had four days off. When they came back in, this pig's head had rotted away, the place stank and there were maggots and bluebottles everywhere. Unsurprisingly, Glen wasn't impressed.

They play pranks in the theatre, but they're a bit tamer than shitting in people's cars. In my first scene in *Fat Friends*, I had to open my lunch box and start eating a bag of crisps. One performance, someone put Tabasco on my crisps. Another performance, I opened my lunch box and saw a fake turd inside. For a second I thought, 'Is Darren Shadford one of the stage crew?'

Anyway, all these pranks jogged the old memory, so I got hold of this fake turd and thought I'd have some fun with it. In the final scene, me and Jodie get married, so I stuffed this fake turd into the bouquet of flowers she was holding, thinking, 'When she throws it at the end, it's going to be brilliant when it lands on someone.' Instead, we were singing to each other in the middle of the stage and this turd fell out of the bouquet and onto the floor with a thud.

Some of the old-stagers were horrified, and people in the front row were pointing at the turd with their hands over their mouths. But Sam Bailey looked like she was about to wet herself and Curly Watts was loving it as well. When the curtain came down, there was an inquest. The tour manager was on the stage, trying to find out who had put the turd in the bouquet, and suddenly what I thought was an innocent prank has turned into a bit of a thing. So I thought, 'Never in the history of musical theatre has anyone seen anything like this, this will be talked about for years, I'm going to own it...' They pulled me into the office and put me in the show report. I felt like saying, 'Jesus, think yourselves lucky, not that long ago it would have been a real one...'

Then again, gone are the days when I could go out after a game, throw eggs at a famous illusionist in a box and carry on the next day as if nothing had happened. That was a weird one. We'd played a game against South Africa, I got clattered at the ground and decided to head out into London. All the lads were in Chinawhite, which was a bit swanky for me and Harmy. I went to the bar, ordered a pint of lager and the barman said, 'We don't do pints, we do small glasses or bottles.' So I bought a couple of small glasses, poured them into my boot and started drinking from it. Not long after that, me and Harmy had been kicked out by the bouncers.

The next morning, my agent phoned and said, 'We've had the *Mirror* on the phone. What were you up to last night?'

'Oh, mate, I got chucked out of Chinawhite for drinking out of my boot. Sorry about that.'

'No, not that. They said you were throwing eggs at David Blaine. You know who I mean, the illusionist bloke, who's sitting in a box suspended above the Thames and is always on the news.'

'Have they got any pictures?'

'No.'

'Great, so I wasn't then...'

To be honest, I'm not sure if I was or not. When you're drinking from your boot in Chinawhite, anything could have happened. But that was the end of it, the story never came out. This was before camera phones were everywhere, and you could get away with behaviour you'd never get away with now. There was only one jape I ever regretted, which involved drinks at the Sri Lanka high commissioner's house, karaoke and Sambuca shots. I can't really tell you the ending, except to say that my mum wouldn't have been proud. Sorry, Bumble.

CHAPTER 12

HARIBO AND TANTRUMS

Celebrity

I have no problem with the Kardashians. You can't really have a go at them. I'm just mystified by all the knobheads who follow them on social media, watch them on telly and buy their stuff, then slag them off on social media. They're not much different to people who moan about footballers being paid tens of millions but who spend 60 quid on a ticket to watch them. If you've got a problem with how much they earn, boycott the matches.

I've heard it said that celebrity adulation is like a religion. If that's the case, Kim Kardashian must be like a modern-day Jesus to some people. I'm not bagging Jesus, but if he wasn't actually the son of God, he was the greatest chancer in history, even bigger than Kim Kardashian. And it would make Jesus the forerunner of Snapchat and Instagram, centuries ahead of his time.

Going in the jungle is the only thing I've ever done for no other reason than the money. But I've got no time for reality TV people and don't really respect them. If my wife turned around and said she wanted to go on *The Real Housewives of Cheshire*, I'd think she wasn't the woman I thought she was.

I'm not going to sit here and judge the people on *The Only Way is Essex* or *Geordie Shore*, they're just trying to make a few quid. It's not for me, but if that's how they want to portray themselves, fair play to them. There's nothing wrong with stacking shelves in a supermarket, but if programme makers want to put these people on TV, make them famous and give them money, then I can see why people would want to do that instead. It's society that's the problem, not them.

For a lot of kids, reality TV has become aspirational TV, which is so sad. They think they don't have to do anything in life to be rewarded. I don't watch *Love Island*, but a lot of people I know watch it. I'll hear people complaining that the world is going to hell in a handcart, and in the next breath they're telling me that they watch *Love Island* every night. Robbie Savage is addicted; every time I see him at the gym he says to me, 'Did you watch *Love Island* last night?' 'No, Robbie, like I said yesterday, and the day before yesterday, and the day before that, I don't watch *Love Island...*' I just think, 'Having sex on TV, just to be famous, is that where we are now?'

I sometimes wonder who are the clever people and who are the idiots? On the one hand, you've got people who make millions by opening boxes on YouTube – 'unboxing', it's called, and there might be a mobile phone or an Xbox or a toy inside – and on the other you've got people who make peanuts by spending months writing books that hardly anyone reads. The people who write books are meant to be the intelligent ones, but there's the conundrum: is slaving over something that you'll be paid very little for cleverer than making millions by pissing about on YouTube? If money is your only measure of success, then yes. Then there are the people who play computer games for a living. They earn millions, fill arenas, and they reckon it will be bigger than actual sport eventually. I've got nothing against the people doing it, they've just found a gap in the market, it's the people watching it I don't get.

One of the things I try to get across to my kids is the importance of having a passion, pursuing it and being the best you can possibly be at whatever that passion might be. Nowadays, people want fame without being good at anything. So I also try to teach my kids that the most important things in life are the hardest to achieve. I've had things handed to me on a plate, and it's given me no satisfaction, not one bit. When I did the musical, I've got no doubt people were saying, 'Why is he doing a musical when he's a former cricketer and can barely sing a note?' But I tried my nuts off, worked so hard to do it to the best of my ability, and that's what made it so worthwhile.

I dipped my toe in the celebrity lifestyle when I was younger, did the rounds, went to the dos in spangly nightclubs, pretended to know people when actually I'd only seen them on TV. Looking back, it was all just a bit weird. I'd go into a room full of celebrities, and someone would approach me and not even bother introducing themselves. Or I'd say, 'I'm Fred, nice to meet you', and they'd say, 'Nice to meet you again.' And I'd be thinking, 'But I've never met you before.' I've been to gatherings where I've mixed people up, because I didn't know who they were. I was in some bar in Mayfair, chatting to this fella, and I was calling him Theo all night and asking him about Arsenal, because I thought he was the footballer Theo Walcott. It was only when I was leaving that someone told me I'd actually been chatting to Marvin from JLS.

Mind you, I have had a couple of moments when I've wanted to use that terrible line, 'Do you know who I am?' I was at Lord's recently, where the kids were playing this indoor tournament. We were walking past the ground with all these other kids and their parents, they were all going on about how wonderful it looked, and I turned around and said, 'I'll give you a tour if you want?' I walked up to the Grace Gates, looked in the hut and realised I didn't know anyone. This woman said, 'Have you got a pass?'

'No, but I'm a life member.'

'Have you got your book on you?'

'No, I've not got me book...'

All the time, I'm looking at her as if to say, 'Come on, love, it's me. You're working at Lord's, you must know who I am...'

But she keeps saying, 'You can't go in if you've not got your pass!'

All the kids and parents are milling about by the gates with excited looks on their faces and there is absolutely no way I can back out, so I say, 'Look, truth be told, I actually used to play a bit for England. I was captain.'

I start looking around for this massive picture of me with a quote next to it, but it's been replaced with one of Andrew Strauss, so I resort to putting my name in Google and saying, 'Look, that's me!'

'You can't go in if you've not got your pass!'

In the end, I ask her to get someone down who might know me, and when this woman turns up who recognises me, I feel like hugging her.

It reminds me of the time me and Darren Gough were trying to get into a nightclub in London. The big Polish lads on the door wouldn't let us in, and as we were trying to persuade them, the Atomic Kittens walked past. Goughie shouted, 'Hey, Kittens, I've been on *This Is Your Life*, I'll go home and get my red book if you like!'

I love Goughie to bits, but I find the whole concept of *This Is Your Life* bonkers. Imagine being sat there in the studio with Michael Aspel and his big red book, and Aspel saying, 'And now, Andrew, it's the two people who brought you into this world and raised you, your mum and dad!' I'd be thinking, 'I was round their house yesterday, having Sunday lunch...'

'And now, Andrew, your best friend Paddy!'

'Oh yeah, I remember Paddy, I was out with him last Friday...'

If there are people I want to see, I'll seem them, I don't need Aspel to track them down for me and reunite us on the telly.

I've got a lot of stories about Goughie and nightclubs, mostly toe-curling. Another time, me and him were walking out the front door, all these cameras started flashing, I ducked out of the way and Goughie started walking towards the paparazzi with his arms outstretched. Turned out they had no idea who we were, they were actually taking pictures of Craig off of *Big Brother*.

People in the entertainment world think they're so impor-tant. Why is that? I just don't get it. I was doing a charity fashion show for Naomi Campbell, standing in the wings listening to three very well-known celebrities, and they were talking about a list that had been published in one of the papers, about the UK's most influential celebrities. Robbie Williams was something like 32nd, and they were having this in-depth discussion about what number he should have been. I was standing there thinking, 'This is really strange.' Then they started talking about meeting up for dinner. One of them turned round to me and said, 'Obviously not you, Fred.' I think it was a joke, although obviously he didn't want me there.

I just thought, 'You know what? I couldn't do it anyway. What would we talk about? Whether you were all as high on the influential celebrity list as you thought you should be?' I'd hate to get to that point, would be so disappointed in myself. The things celebrities get hung up on is just bizarre. The way some of them talk, they seem to think they're curing the world of all evils, one laugh at a time. When I'm abseiling down some building or other, or dressed in drag, performing cabaret in Paris, the thought that I might be making some-one's day a little bit better is the only real crumb of comfort I can cling on to.

It was a real eye-opener working in TV for the first time, it's just the weirdest environment ever. Suddenly all these people are brown-nosing you and you can't do anything wrong. It's the strangest feeling. After one of the first episodes of *A League of Their Own*, I came off set and people were saying, 'Fred! Brilliant show!'

'But I didn't say owt.'

'But what you did say was amazing!'

'No, but seriously, I didn't do anything...'

People were running around all over the place, pandering to my every need, fetching us cups of tea and cans of Coke, and I was thinking, 'I can make a cup of tea myself. The kettle's just over there. Why don't I make it myself?' And because runners will do anything for you, treat you like little tin gods just because you happen to be appearing on a TV show, some of the little tin gods will take advantage, treat the runners like servants.

People believing their own hype really bothers me, because the real talent is the people who come up with the ideas and put the shows together. Cameramen, producers, the people doing the technical jobs, they're doing the nitty-gritty, the little tin gods just turn up, read autocues and talk nonsense.

You'll be on set and there'll be more food than in a supermarket, just in case you fancy three bags of Haribo or a whole lemon drizzle cake between filming. I did one acting job, was standing around waiting to do my thing, and it started to rain a bit. Bang, all of a sudden there was a girl standing next to me, holding a brolly over my head. I said to her, 'It's fine, give me the brolly, I can do it.' And she replied, 'No, I've got to do it, it's part of my job.' Being a runner is having a foot on the ladder, so they're entitled to take their job seriously. But I also understand why famous people turn into such pricks and lose all sense of perspective because absolutely everything is done for them.

I've seen tantrums, people storming off set. Some people in the entertainment industry are so precious that they think the normal rules of civility don't apply to them. There will be hissy fits left, right and centre, because someone has contradicted them or given an opinion that doesn't tally exactly with theirs. Because they're in front of camera and 'the talent', they're right and therefore everybody else must be wrong. In any other world it wouldn't be tolerated, but in TV it is. You'll be filming in the street, somebody will walk into shot and they'll get shouted at as if they're the worst human being ever. People are just going about their everyday business, walking to the shops or off to catch a bus, we're the ones doing something weird.

Then you get the people who say, 'Be nice to the runners on your way up, because they might be your boss one day.' And I'll think, 'What's that got to do with anything? Are you suggesting that if you get the impression a runner is never going to work in TV again you can treat them like shit?' Just be nice to them, say please and thank you, because it's the right thing to do, not because there might be something in it for you a few years down the line.

What I also don't like about TV is the fact it's so subjective. In sport (unless it's something like dressage – there's no way dancing horses should be in the Olympics), if you play well you keep getting picked, if you play badly you get dropped. But in TV, one commissioner might like you, another might not. I hate the fact you're powerless and it's all so random. Every now and again, I'll apply for a gig in TV and know I'm the best person for the job, but some woman or bloke will like someone else. That really annoys me. I can't deal with subjectivity; with everything in life there's a right and a wrong way.

I'll watch a show and think, 'Why have they not got rid of him?' Or I'll watch *Homes Under the Hammer* and think, 'Why is Dion Dublin on it?' I used to like *Homes Under the Hammer*, but he's ruined it. When I watched *Homes Under the Hammer*, I never once thought, 'You know what this programme needs? An ex-professional footballer who's got absolutely no interest in a two-up, two-down in Colchester.' Martin and Lucy were doing perfectly well without Dion

Dublin. When Dion's walking around some house that's just been bought for £80 grand at auction, and he's telling me it needs a downstairs toilet, I can tell he doesn't really care. But people probably watch me on programmes and think, 'Why is Fred Flintoff on this? Get rid of him!'

A lot of the trappings of celebrity are wasted on me. I only ever wanted to be a cricketer, and everything that's come since is a bonus. When I played in Soccer Aid, I didn't have any nerves, even though we were playing in front of almost 80,000 people. I never had any aspirations to be a footballer, so why would I be nervous? Playing at Old Trafford was a privilege, but it was a charity match, not a full international! That's where people get it wrong. It didn't matter if Usain Bolt skinned me and scored (he did skin me once, but never again...) When it came to the penalties, I was fine with it. I just placed it, bottom corner. No idea who the goalkeeper was. Someone from Westlife?

I don't really get star-struck, unless it's cricketers. I was star-struck when I played against Sachin Tendulkar for the first time and when I met Viv Richards, who is the coolest man on the planet. The Queen was very nice. She said to me, 'I see you have a racehorse running at Carlisle tomorrow. Has it a chance?' I said, 'Yes, it's worth a couple of quid, Your Majesty.' I had dinner with Archbishop Desmond Tutu, when we got lifetime memberships at Lord's on the same day. Funnily enough, he reminded me of the fella from the sitcom *Desmond's*, he had the same infectious laugh and was the life and soul of the party. I went to a David Beckham World Cup party, and as he was coming around the table with his mate, I was thinking, 'I know that fella from somewhere.' Then I twigged it was Puff Daddy. When he got to me, I said, 'All right, Puff?', and I could see Beckham wincing. Puff replied, 'My name is Sean'.

But you know what they say about meeting your heroes. When I was 19, I went to a dinner with Ian Botham, who was a big hero of mine when I was growing up. I loved the way he went about things, made things happen, wanted to be involved in the big moments in the game. It was a boozy night, during which we drank copious amounts of wine and listened to Botham hold court. Afterwards, me and Botham were walking down the street arm in arm, and I was thinking, 'This is unbelievable, I'm walking down the street arm in arm with Ian Botham – Sir Ian Botham! – someone pinch me.'

We got back to the hotel and he invited me up to his suite for a nightcap. By that point I'd have done pretty much anything Botham had asked me to do. One drink turned into two turned into three until we were really quite battered. But the night came to an abrupt and undignified end when Botham leant down to get some more drinks, got a bit of a heavy head and fell through the TV. I made my excuses – 'Night, Ian, I'll leave you to it' – while he was still precariously balanced on top of the mini-bar.

The kids went to school in Alderley Edge in Cheshire for a while, and the yard would be full of footballers every day. Wayne Rooney, Robin van Persie, Vincent Kompany. But because I'm not into football, I wasn't bothered. One day I was waiting for the kids, Les Dennis came walking past, and I was like, 'Les Dennis! It's Les Dennis!' I used to watch him on the telly when I was a kid, when he was absolutely cracking it. If I met Michael Palin, I'd be the same, because I watched all his shows when he was travelling all over the world. I save my adulation for people who do stuff that means something to me and do it well.

And if someone famous annoys me, I won't give them the time of day. I got invited to go on *Parkinson* and said no, because I didn't fancy it. Actually, there's a bit more to it than that. When we were playing against South Africa in 2003, we had Parky's radio show on in the dressing room one lunchtime, and he hammered all of us. Then when I started doing well, he wanted me on his show. Oh no, Parky, it doesn't work like that. I've got a stubbornness about me, once I'd got it into my head that I'd never go on his show, that was the end of it.

I'm impressed by anyone who works hard to excel at their job. When I was doing the musical, I'd watch Jodie Prenger sing and dance and act, and be absolutely blown away. I could tell she'd done everything she possibly could to perform to the best of her ability, poured all her passion into that production, and that's what gave her the edge.

I was also in awe of Mike Tyson, who came and watched a sparring session before I had my boxing match. He got off his tour bus with his entourage and I thought, 'This is gonna be a flying visit, they'll get him on camera arriving and then he'll be off', but he spent about an hour in the gym. When he walked in, the atmosphere completely changed. When he started speaking, everyone was hanging on his every word. I know about the bad things he's done, but he spoke with passion about boxing and life and I didn't want him to leave. I love that he made something of himself, despite his awful upbringing, and there was this strange insecurity, innocence and vulnerability about him. I gravitate towards flawed people, because there's an authenticity about them. Listening to Tyson made me think, 'You know what, I could do something great as well.'

But someone doesn't have to be famous to impress me. It might be someone who can build a house, fix my car when it's gone wrong or teach kids with learning disabilities. Or my dad, who can fit windows or help build an extension. I'm disappointed by famous people I meet all the time. You'll get celebrities or sportspeople trying to lecture you or trying to be profound. But because they're trying so hard to be profound, it has the opposite effect. People will tell you how humble they are, but other people are supposed to tell them that. Chances are, if you're having to tell people you're humble, you're not.

CHAPTER 13

CHIPS, BEANS AND LAMBORGHINIS

The simple things

I like to think I still have working-class values, but I can't really claim to be working-class if I've got a Ferrari out the front and a Lamborghini in the garage. And when you're not born into privilege, there is a guilt attached to having money. I get embarrassed turning up to certain places in the Ferrari, especially if I go back to Preston to see some old mates. Or I'll worry about old mates coming round my house. But I'm not really sure what I'm meant to do. It's strange, because half of me worries that people will think I'm flash, but the other half of me likes driving a nice car and living in a nice house. It confuses me a little bit. Even writing this is difficult. I don't want to come across as one of those dicks always going on about how humble they are. At the same time, I don't want to come across as enjoying my wealth too much. I feel like I can't win.

I'm happy in my own little world, with people I feel at home with. And I'm at my most comfortable with the lads I used to go drinking with at the social club. To them, I'm not a cricketer or a person off the telly, I'm just a lad they knew as a kid who's done all right. Apart from Robbie Savage, who I speak to almost every day, I don't knock around with anybody from the entertainment world, because I haven't really got anything in common with them. I've got my mates in Preston, Paddy, Steve – who drives me up and down the country and who I spend a ridiculous amount of time with. I've got Keysey and Harmy from the cricket, but I don't have a bank of cricketing pals from around the world.

I had a close group of friends at Lancashire, but when you retire from sport, your world just stops, while their lives carry on as before. Someone else takes your place in the team and suddenly he's getting all the invites to teammates' weddings and birthday parties. I moved to Dubai, and then to Surrey, because I wanted to escape that life. Everything had been turned upside down, I had no idea what I wanted to do. That meant losing contact with a lot of people. Then when I started doing the TV stuff, some people thought I'd dumped them, and was spending all my time hanging out with celebrities instead. What they didn't understand was that I stopped being around them or phoning them up because they reminded me of what I still desperately wanted. I felt bad for a while, but then I thought, 'Hang on a minute, why did nobody phone me? I'm the one who's retired because of a knackered knee at the age of thirty-one, I need a bit of a hug. And I've only stopped playing cricket, I'm not dead.'

I bump into cricket folk and speak to them, but the problem with cricket people is that all they want to talk about is cricket. I've fallen back in love with it, I love watching my boys play and I love talking about it, but not all the time. I don't work in cricket in any capacity, so I don't really know what's going on. Plus, I'm not that bothered about knowing the nuts and bolts of the game.

I feel like a fish out of water at parties and functions, because I find the chat that so-called high-flying people come out with boring. I put the barriers up, because I just can't be arsed with it. Sometimes someone will say to me, 'I can't work you out.' 'Why are you trying to work me out? Why do you have to know how I work? I'm not trying to work you out because I don't care. And I'm not even sure I've figured myself out yet. What I do know is that I don't want to be anywhere near this party.' It's all about what people have got, the conversations are superficial bullshit. I just want conversation with normal people who talk about normal things, not the boat they just bought, the famous people they've been hanging out with, which famous person is seeing which other famous person or who's said what about who.

When I'm doing telly, I'm putting a face on. Literally. I've realised that when you're on TV – especially now everything's in HD – you have to at least try to look half-decent, so I've upped my game since I stopped playing cricket. Robbie Savage gave me some thickening powder for my hair, and I've started blow-drying it. I had it cut recently and the woman made a complete hash of it. I got more upset than I thought I would, and it got me thinking, 'If I went bald, what would I do?' Maybe I'd have a transplant, like Shane Warne. Then again, look at Russ Abbot, he's been bald as a coot for years and doesn't give a shit.

I'm part of the design process with Jacamo. I sit around the table with the proper designers, discussing the 'mood boards', they tell me what the new fashions are going to be, I tell them what I'd like to wear, and we meet halfway. I don't want my range to be high-end fashion, and it's not like I've turned into Karl Lagerfeld, but I'm more aware of what I put on in the morning. Knocking about with Jamie Redknapp hasn't helped. He makes you think about aspects of fashion you really shouldn't be thinking about. Jamie knows more about fashion than Giorgio Armani. I went clothes shopping with him once. Never again.

I do sometimes look at myself in the mirror and heave a big sigh, but I do a lot more male grooming now. I did a promo for a grooming company, and I was surrounded by my make-up man Donald, a stylist, my agent, my driver Steve, a security person, and all I could think was, 'How did I get here? Who am I? What have I become?' But I'm comfortable with those people, I trust them. I have a good laugh with Donald and Steve, which is important, because when I get on camera, I want to be relaxed.

'Relaxed' is not a word that springs to mind when I think about my one and only brush with colonic irrigation. I had to lose weight quick, because weighing day was coming up with England. A mate recommended it, I did some research and it looked like it might do the trick.

There's a clinic in Hale, and I booked under the name of Trevor Jesty, a former Lancashire player and umpire, because I didn't want them to know it was me. I'm sat there in the waiting room, surrounded by all these women, and a girl comes out and says, 'Mr Jesty, we're ready for you now.' I don't move, but because I'm the only bloke in there, all these women are looking at me. The girl says, 'Mr Jesty, are you ready for your irrigation?' Now all these women are looking at me knowing I'm about to get a pipe stuck up my clacker.

I go into this room and the girl says, 'Right, lie on the bed and put your knees up.' She gets this pipe out and plugs it in, so to speak, and starts asking me how I feel. I reply, 'Lovely, cracking, really nice.' She turns the tap on and says, 'Tell me when you can't take any more and I'll turn it off.' I'm lying there thinking, 'How much is acceptable? Should I be taking two litres? Ten litres?' When my eyes feel like they're swimming, I start shouting, 'Enough! Enough!'

She turns it off, pulls out this shaving mirror and says, 'You can watch what comes out.' So I start pushing it out and it feels like I'm pooing the bed, while she's rubbing my tummy and chatting as if it's the most normal thing in the world.

As I'm watching this brown water running through the pipe, she says, 'Are you a fast eater?'

'Yes, I am, I love my food and chuck it down.'

'You can tell. Did you have Sunday lunch this week?'

'Yeah.'

'Well, there's a carrot, there's a bit of beef...'

I was dying inside. She filled me up and flushed me out again and let me go. But what do you say as a way of goodbye to a woman who has just stuck a pipe up your clacker and given you a running commentary of your Sunday lunch leaving your body? When I weighed myself, it hadn't made a bit of difference.

Another thing I'll never have again is a massage. I gave up on massages after a tour of Pakistan. I went into this room, got stripped off, lay on the bed and this fella started slapping me on the forehead. I thought, 'Ignore it, this is just what they do in these parts.' But when he switched to my legs, things got a bit awkward. He made his way up my thighs and suddenly – Ding! – flicked my balls. I didn't know whether to hit him or kiss him.

One of the reasons I enjoy doing the podcast, probably more than anything else I do, is because I don't have to worry about what I look like, so I can just rock up in a hoodie and a pair of shorts. Second, I just sit around in a studio with Robbie, who's one of my best mates, and Matthew, who has also become a really good friend, and talk about whatever we fancy. The producers, Michael and Stanley, are nice to be around, which is more important to me than the money, and I don't know what's going to happen every time we do it. We don't rehearse anything, and if we get into a subject that seems worth exploring, we'll run with it. We do it on a Monday, talk until we reach a natural conclusion, and then the producers do what they do and release it the same day.

Usually, the first thing that comes out of your mouth is truly what you believe, so while I do take it seriously in my own way, I don't like to give it too much thought beforehand. It allows me to have a say on a wide variety of subjects, but not in any official capacity. It's not the same as doing an interview with a journalist or saying something as a pundit. When we started doing it, the editor kept taking bits out, because it's the BBC and they err on the side of caution. But my point was, if you're telling a story and there's something a bit risqué in it, it's the risqué bit that's usually the crux of the story. If you start taking the risqué bits out, you might as well not bother. So now we keep the risqué bits in, and it seems to have worked.

I have to have a public persona, because I'm quite quiet, I don't really speak. That wouldn't work too well on *A League of Their Own*, just sitting there for half an hour, saying nothing, week after week. The only time I didn't really have to put on a persona was in *I'm a Celeb*. I could tell that other people in the jungle were putting on an act because they thought that would make the public see them in a better light, but you can only keep that up for so long. After a period of time, you revert to type and become yourself again.

Take work out of the equation and my life is quite simple. It's not simple enough at the moment, but I'm getting there. I know a lot of people, but I've not got many proper mates. Even the mates I do have I never phone up just for a chat. I could quite easily become a recluse. That's one of the reasons I like travelling on planes. I don't like the queuing-up bit, but once you're on it, you've got your food and movies and nobody can get to you. That's also why we've moved to where we have, a small town in Cheshire. I'll walk to the gym, potter around the market, see my mates back in Preston every now and again, and that's about it. The rest of my time is spent with the family.

I don't buy a newspaper and don't really watch the news. I used to watch *Corrie* all the time, grew up on it, but it's gone a bit daft, people are dying every week. I watch *Take Me Out* with the kids on a Saturday night – 'No lighty, no likey' – it should be rubbish but it's brilliant. I tried explaining it to Matthew Syed once and it was like teaching early man about the concept of the wheel. I watch a bit of cricket, but mainly box sets, although I'm a bit over *Game of Thrones*. The first series was good, mainly because of Sean Bean. You know where you are with Sean Bean – the North! Bean won't put on an accent for anyone: this is him, this is how he speaks, live with it. The rest of it, all those dragons and fantasy stuff, is a bit fancy for me. I watch other stuff, like *Breaking Bad*, and don't know if I enjoy them or not. If you don't get me in the first ten minutes, I'm done. But if I get past those first ten minutes and get sucked in, it becomes something I've got to do, like a mission. If I start something, I have to finish it, whether it's a box set or a giant bag of Doritos.

My attention span is bad and, although it sounds terrible, people bore me. I'm better with animals and kids. I can't do inane chat. Dinner parties – what's the point? It's just people talking for the sake of talking, because they happen to be sat around a table. I'm exaggerating. But only slightly.

People have holiday friends, but I don't understand the point of them. If they're that much fun, why don't you see them all the time, instead of once a year in Tenerife? 'Mick and Sue are going to back to Tenerife this summer, shall we?' No! I go on holiday because I don't want to see my friends for a week, I don't want to pick up any new ones. Sometimes I wonder how I make any friends in the first place.

Certain social situations kill me. I can't stand weddings, because you end up being trapped on a table with people I don't know. They think it's genius to make the seating plan boy-girl, boy-girl, but why would I want to sit next to some strange woman? Sometimes I'll turn up early and move the names around, so that I'm sitting next to someone I already know. It's not just the bride and groom's day, it's my day as well! I've made the effort to come, taken time off work, paid for flights and a hotel, and now you want me to sit next to a stranger? That's not going to happen.

And you want a present! Wedding lists are the cheekiest things I've seen in my life. I understood it back in the day, when people were moving in together and genuinely needed pots and pans and cutlery. But nowadays, people have holiday vouchers. I'm not paying for you to go on holiday!

If you want to go on holiday, go on holiday, you earn £100 grand a year!

I might have a few mates round for the boxing, get a curry in, which I enjoy, but I like my house to be for me. It's my castle, my domain. I can't have it when people stay over, and I don't like staying over at other people's houses. Why would I want to stay in another person's house? It's awkward, I'd sooner stay in a hotel. There's too much pressure to do the right thing in another person's house. You've got to ask to have a drink or get something out of the fridge. I don't need the aggravation, I'd sooner phone room service.

And whoever invented the downstairs loo needs shooting. Taking a dump is one of the most natural things you can do, but it's fraught with danger, especially when the downstairs toilet is just off the lounge. You'll be in there, running the taps, coughing, anything to cover up the sound of you having this massive dump, and the whole time you're worrying about the smell, whether you'll be able to get rid of it and whether it will follow you out. Toilets on aeroplanes are even worse, because you're taking a dump about two feet away from people preparing food or eating their tea, and when you open the door, the smell trails out after you like a creeping fog.

The whole concept of toilet seats is wrong. You wander into a service station toilet, pull your pants and trousers down, rest your cheeks on a seat that someone else's sweaty arse was resting on just seconds earlier, unleash everything you've got, wipe your arse and pull your pants and trousers back on. Seconds later, someone else goes in and does exactly the same thing. Repeat and repeat. I'd rather just do it in a hole in the ground, at least then I wouldn't have to deal with someone winking at me as they come out of the trap, as if to say, 'That might be the best dump I've ever done – follow that...'

Things that other people think are brilliant, I don't. Getting a backstage pass to meet someone famous at a festival doesn't excite me in the slightest. People would kill to play football at Old Trafford, but I'm honestly not bothered. I don't know whether it's my northern upbringing, but I've still got an idea of what things should cost and won't pay more than that, whether it's a pair of trainers or a T-shirt. I buy some things and feel really guilty. If I spent a fortune on a pair of jeans, I think I'd be scared to wear them. I was happy with my free chinos from Reiss, and when my missus shrank them, I was gutted. I even get excited when I see a tub of half-price Haagen-Dazs ice cream in a petrol garage. I'll be clutching it with a big grin on my face, like a metal detectorist who's just unearthed an ancient artefact.

I like cycling and have a few bikes in the garage, but I've probably done about 5,000 miles on my old bike from Halfords.

When I was in Australia, someone gave me this fancy bike with deep-set wheels and electric gears, but on the couple of occasions I've taken it out, I've felt like a proper bellend. People say, 'Oh, but this bike is lighter.' I'm 16 stone, for God's sake! As if a bike that's two pounds lighter is going to make any difference to how I cycle. I could put a load of bricks on my back and it wouldn't make much difference. And anyway, I go out on my bike for training, so I don't want it to be easy, I want it to be hard!

I'll admit to being a bit of a contradiction, because while I'm not really into material things, I do like my cars. I've only driven the Lamborghini three times since I bought it. It's a slightly older one, an investment, and I look at it and think, 'That's a nice car.' But, let's be honest: a car only makes you happy for about ten minutes. You drive a Lamborghini a couple of times and it just becomes a car, like any other car, except with an annoyingly loud engine.

The Lambo is a complete nightmare. I have to put two pieces of wood on my drive to get it out, because it's too steep. When I get in it, my head sticks out the top, so I look like one of the Ant Hill Mob from *Wacky Races*, or Hightower from *Police Academy*. I'm constantly on the lookout for potholes, and I'm paranoid about kerbing it. When I try to use the indicator, it gets stuck on my knee. I can't see the satnav because it's hidden behind my legs. I had to get my hair cut short because my fringe kept getting squashed. The seats are carbon, so my arse gets wedged in and I need a tin opener to get out. When I pull up anywhere, I look like a total knobhead. I have to press this button, move the door up with my elbow, and as I'm climbing out, I look like a giraffe having a drink. If I took it to the supermarket, I could probably fit a small bottle of milk and a loaf of bread in the boot, which is at the front of the car and took me about three weeks to work out how to open. I only bought it because Robbie Savage kept telling me how great it was. Then he started hammering me, for not being a man of the people. It's the best and worst thing I've ever bought.

Grand gestures and big gifts and words are wasted on me. When I saw Victoria Falls, I thought, 'That's nice, a big waterfall. What next?' When I saw the Taj Mahal, I thought, 'Wow, that is amazing.' But the excitement wore off quickly. After looking at it for five minutes, I thought, 'What next?' But I'll travel on the Tube in London, get off at the right stop and want to high-five someone. Someone will give me the smallest of presents, or one of my kids will say something, and it will make me so happy. For the rest of the day I'll be thinking, 'That was amazing.' I find simple things so much more powerful.

I've been so fortunate to travel the world, do all sorts of weird and wonderful things, stay in the best hotels and eat in the best restaurants. And I enjoy eating in nice restaurants. But I'm more comfortable with what I grew up with. I had a roast at a Toby Carvery recently – four meats, a mountain of veg, a bucket of gravy – and it was better than any posh restaurant I've ever eaten in. But when I tweeted a picture of it, there were food snobs slagging it off, saying how unsophisticated I was, eating at a Toby Carvery.

Fish fingers, chips and beans with the family is the best meal in the world. And some of the best times I have are when we're all sat around together, cuddled up on the couch, watching something on TV, with everyone laughing. That's better than playing for England. I look around, not at the stuff in the house, but at my family, and think, 'You know what, you've done all right.'

When I was younger, I thought things like fast cars would make me happy and that success was measured by how much you earned and how big your house was. That's what society leads us to believe. But I worked out pretty early that money doesn't buy you happiness. My first wage with Lancashire was £2,500 a year and I thought I was minted. By my late teens I was earning decent money, so I bought a house and a couple of cars, so I could take my mates out. I wanted them to be happy, but I wasn't happy.

I wasn't very good with money, didn't care how much I spent on a night out and didn't really take the taxman into account. So I ended up losing it all. I sold the house and the cars and was on the verge of bankruptcy until my agent at the time, Chubby Chandler, paid my tax bill. I still had nothing, so I moved back with my mum and dad and got myself back on my feet. And suddenly I was happy again. Remember what I was saying earlier about feeling content in uncomfortable situations? It makes me feel alive.

I know people who are so wealthy it's ridiculous, but they're not happy, because someone else has three quid more than them, is going on a better holiday or driving a faster car. It's all about social climbing and competition, peering over the garden fence and getting irritated that your neighbour's garden is bigger than yours. I played with people like that and know people now in the celebrity world who will never be happy because they suspect someone else is doing better. I find it difficult to understand, because I want all my mates to crack it and be happy doing what they're doing.

Being a nice person and comfortable in yourself are the two most important things in life. Otherwise, what's the point? When your head hits the pillow at night or you look in the mirror in the morning, what else have you got if you're not decent and content? If you had asked me ten years ago, 'What would you like to change about yourself?', my reply would have lasted about ten minutes. But now I'm happier, more relaxed than I've ever been. I've accepted who I am. Or, perhaps more accurately, I've resigned myself to being me.

CHAPTER 14

A BEE IN
ME BONNET

Things that get my goat

Just as I can't stand people kissing arse, I can't handle rudeness, it makes my blood boil. Dishonesty really gets me as well. If somebody stitches me up, they're done, it's non-negotiable. Through the years, I've had plenty of people use me to climb the social ladder. People I thought were friends have used me and then dropped me. I won't name them, but I hope they get found out.

I've also been betrayed by teammates, coaches and financial advisors. Sportspeople are easy prey, quite naive in a lot of ways. When I retired from cricket at 31, I'd never paid any bills, that was all done for me. I was a sucker, used to lend money to friends willy-nilly and throw myself into things. My money was invested for me, a lot of it in shit. There was a flat in

Turnberry I didn't even know I owned. I was involved in schemes for this, that and the other, none of which I had any knowledge of.

These financial advisors come to your wedding and your children's christenings and are meant to be your mates. Where I live now, I see all these people – businessmen, estate agents, women – trying to get money out of footballers, offering once-in-a-lifetime 'opportunities'. They tap into them and try to bleed them dry. That's why footballers are so guarded, don't want to speak to the public or the press, in case they give anything away. It's only when I retired that I started unravelling all the mistakes that had been made on my behalf, and now I'm always looking for catches and ulterior motives.

I had an uneasy relationship with the press when I was playing. I hated being interviewed. I found it pointless, because you could never say what you really wanted to say. The truth rarely seemed like the best option. The press liaison officer would tell you what the journalists were going to ask you and provide you with the correct answers and what not to say. But looking back, I wish I'd just ignored them and been more honest. If you give an honest opinion, it can't be wrong. If you played rubbish, say you played rubbish.

I'm fed up with sportspeople taking the positives out of everything. If you got hammered on the field, one person scoring a few runs or taking a couple of wickets aren't positives, because it's a team game and you were well beaten. That's the bottom line. I did it myself, because I was told to, and I hated myself for it. When I was captain and we got beaten – again – I just wanted to say, 'You know what? We were absolutely rubbish.' But I had to drag the positives out of it, even though there were none. Now, I listen to them on the telly, talking about taking the positives from a 4–0 defeat in Australia, and I tear my hair out. Let them go a little bit. Just say something real. Be honest.

I was suspicious of cricket journalists. They weren't the best of people and I didn't like half of them. I'd sit in front of them and they were always trying to be clever, because they were after an angle. I tried answering in-depth, I tried ignoring people, but soon realised there was no best way of dealing with it. I got on with some of them, but only to a point. If I don't trust people, I struggle to engage with them on any level. One minute the press would be all over me, proclaiming me to be the best thing since sliced bread, the next they'd be selling me down the river, just to sell a few more copies of whatever paper they worked for. I know they were only doing their job, but some of the stuff wasn't doing their job, it was just unpleasant.

After I was involved in the pedalo incident in the Caribbean in 2007 – when I was spotted dragging a pedalo into the sea in St Lucia, at 3 a.m., in the middle of a World Cup – I was genuinely embarrassed. I got a bollocking from Duncan Fletcher and when I was called in to do this press conference, to explain my behaviour, I had to walk through hotel reception, where all these England fans were gathered, and I couldn't make eye contact with any of them.

I realised I'd done wrong, and was very low about it, but after being grilled by all these journalists, I thought, 'They're having a crack at me for trying to get in a pedalo, but I've seen you lot hammered, men in your forties and fifties, behaving awfully, being rude and obnoxious, speaking to people like shit, falling over on the beach, so why are you judging me for my behaviour?' Talk about flying the flag for their country. I get that they're not playing cricket for England, but they are representing England through their publications, aren't they?

They'd bash out their 500 words as quick as they could after a day's play so they could get away for dinner with their mates, and then turn up the next morning with a hangover, not knowing what was going on – what the pitch was going to do or how the weather might change the playing conditions. I'd listen to pundits and commentators and they wouldn't understand what was being bowled, or they'd not know the players, or just talk for the sake of talking. I found it annoying when pundits and journalists were ill-informed or just plain incorrect. Sometimes they got it right – and I'd tell them if they got it right – but if you're having to churn out pieces every day, you're going to get things wrong. There were real double-standards, and I hated the hypocrisy.

When I announced my retirement on the final day of the County Championship, they claimed I'd done it on purpose, to steal the limelight. Then, in the next sentence, they were writing nice things again. I found it cowardly. If you think I'm a dick, don't start pretending you don't, at least see it through to the end. I had a go at a couple of journalists in press conferences and they're even more precious than sportspeople. They'd get all shirty, and I'd think, 'Hang on a minute, you can criticise me, but I can't criticise something you've written?' Who do they think they are? I've blocked most of them on Twitter, because I don't need them in my life.

As a sportsperson, you're expected to know everything in your late teens or early twenties. Obviously, you don't. In almost any other job, by the time you get to the top of your profession, you've got half a life's experience behind you. But in sport, you're expected to be the finished article, physically and mentally, when you're still really young. Your life drastically changes, you suddenly get all this attention and money and fame, and it's a very difficult thing to deal with. People make mistakes in all walks of life, but when you're a famous sportsperson, people are lying in wait, ready to jump all over you.

It's the tall poppy syndrome we're famous for in Britain: they build you up and end up hammering you. But writing a scathing, negative story is easier than writing a good one. The same journalist who had a swipe at me for floundering after retiring from cricket attacked my BBC podcast colleague Matthew Syed on Twitter. I thought, 'Hang on a minute, mate, this bloke you're attacking is one of the best writers in the country, someone who travels the world giving lectures to all these blue-chip companies, a man who knows his stuff inside-out, and you're taking pot shots at him from the sidelines.'

It's sad that journalists, ex-players (who are often twice as good in retirement as they actually were) and people on social media try to make a name for themselves by having a go at other people. I feel sorry for anybody who spends their days having a pop at people on Twitter. Is their life that bad that the only way they can make themselves feel better is by denigrating other people's achievements? I imagine them to be blokes sat in their flats surrounded by cats, eating a Pot Noodle followed by a Caramac and swigging on a bottle of Tizer. If you can't make a name for yourself, tough, but don't try to stay relevant or gain an extra few readers or Twitter followers by being horrible to other people.

I thought the fallout from the Aussie ball-tampering scandal was embarrassing. Ball-tampering has been going on for years. It's a batter's game, why not let the bowlers have a bit of an advantage for once? Sucking sweets and rubbing your saliva on the ball, throwing the ball into the dirt, lifting the seam, it's all ball-tampering. The Aussies took it a bit further, but more than anything else, I just thought they were a bit thick. It was just ridiculously stupid, taking sandpaper on and giving it to the young kid to do. Yellow sandpaper! At least make sure it's white or hide it on your thumb.

What got me was this idea that nobody else in the Aussie team knew, apart from the captain Steve Smith, the vice-captain David Warner and Cameron Bancroft, the kid who was caught doing it. Give me a break. Anyone with that ball in their hand, reverse-swinging it all over the place, would have known what was going on. If not, I feel sorry for them, because they must have thought they were genuinely as good as Wasim Akram, my old Lancashire teammate, who used to be able to bend a ball around corners. It's like driving a car, turning the power steering on and claiming you don't notice.

But what annoyed me more than the actual ball-tampering was the reaction to it. I was embarrassed for some of the people I'd played with, it was awful hearing old teammates trying to raise their profile on the back of other people's misery. That's another reason why I didn't go down the punditry route, because I didn't want to be that person.

I also can't pretend that I'm that bothered about things that happen in cricket. Someone will get picked for England and pundits will write these angry articles. But I'm never going to say, 'Fuckin' 'ell, I cannot believe Adil Rashid has been picked for England, I am absolutely furious about it. Where's my pen? I must tell everyone exactly how angry I am in a newspaper article.' Who gives a shit whether Adil Rashid gets picked for England or not? Get over it, Geoffrey Boycott!

When I saw Steve Smith crying his eyes out on TV, I put out a tweet saying, 'Happy now? Is this what you wanted?' It was similar to when Pakistan's Mohammad Amir was banned for spot-fixing, for bowling no-balls. It was dreadful, but he was a vulnerable 17-year-old kid who came from nothing, was still getting paid peanuts, was easily influenced and got involved in something he shouldn't. That didn't matter to some people, but I wanted him to have a second chance to redeem himself, and thankfully he has.

What also got me was the sanctimony and the lack of empathy. I direct messaged Steve Smith on Twitter while it was all going on, because I felt for him. I interviewed him when I was working on *The Project* in Australia, and he's a nice, polite lad. He got it wrong, but I've made mistakes too.

He's not Robert Mugabe, he hasn't murdered anyone. I also like Darren Lehmann, but David Warner I struggle to have sympathy for.

Not long after Ben Stokes was banned by England for having a punch-up outside a nightclub, I found myself in a similar situation in Milton Keynes. I'd just done a show, was heading towards the hotel – Lenny Henry's house, Premier Inn – and two lads came up to me. One of them got right in my face and slapped me, so I grabbed the top of his head and pushed it on the pavement. While I had him down, I said to his mate, 'Don't even think about it, because you'll get it as well.' As I was saying it, I was thinking about what had happened to Ben, and how it could go horribly wrong for me as well.

So I said, 'Mate, when I let go of your head, I want you to walk away, because if you don't, this is gonna end badly.' Luckily, because I hadn't been drinking, I was thinking clearly. There was CCTV everywhere and I didn't want to hit him anyway, I couldn't think of anything worse. Thankfully, as soon as I released the bloke on the floor, they both scurried off. When I got to my room, I looked at myself in the mirror and thought, 'What is wrong with me? I'm six foot four, had a professional boxing fight and that little Herbert thought he could have a pop at me? Maybe I need a neck tattoo?' A couple of days later, he sent me an apology email and said he deserved a black eye. Maybe I missed a trick.

I've seen the footage of Ben, and the last ten seconds didn't look good. And as a professional sportsperson, you've got to be careful about the situations you put yourself in. I'm not an aggressive person and I don't know why anyone would want to have a fight, at least in the street. For me to have a fight, someone would have to hit me first, or I'd have to be protecting someone. I think Ben is that kind of person. If anyone has a go at any of his mates, he'll be the first man in there. That's what he's like on a cricket field, and that's one of the reasons he's the great player he is.

What irritated me was that I had journalists phoning me up, trying to equate what he did to my pedalo incident. I wasn't having it. I tried to get in a plastic boat, I didn't lump anyone. And there were the usual suspects in the media, ex-players making all sorts of assumptions, promoting their views on social media, even while the police investigation was still going on.

I struggled with snides as a player. You don't have to get on with everyone in your team, but it helps if everyone trusts each other. That wasn't the case with the England teams I played in. In 2005, when the public and the press assumed we all got on like a house on fire, I reckon I trusted about eight of my team-mates. The other three, nah.

When I started playing for England, the dressing room wasn't a friendly place and I felt like an outsider. It was awful, very disappointing. Michael Atherton, who I knew from Lancashire, was great, took me out for dinner with a reporter called Michael Henderson, who was a bit of a character and one of the few I actually liked. But when I first walked into the dressing room with my big bag, nobody moved. Everyone had their own spots where they changed, so I ended up next door, with the washing machines. Goughie was brilliant, as was his fellow bowler Angus Fraser, who's a great man. Some of the others, not so much.

At the time, England were rubbish, as they had been for most of the eighties and nineties. They never won owt. I'd watch them get hammered by Australia, they'd win one Test to make it 4–1 and celebrate like they'd won the Ashes back. It would make me cringe. 'Boys, you've won one game. The Aussies already had their feet up, because they won the Ashes weeks ago.' Despite that, some of the former players swan around as if they are all-time greats. They pontificate, criticise current players and harp on about how it was so much better in their day. The bowlers were faster, the batters were tougher, there were more characters. Problem was, lads, you didn't win much! So many of these players are revered, but if I could choose any of them to play in the 2005 Ashes-winning team, I'd probably only have Gooch. (I couldn't have Botham, because that would mean me missing out!)

They were so insecure, there was more competition in the dressing room than out on the field. Andrew Caddick was jealous of Goughie, and they were supposed to be working in perfect harmony as our new-ball partnership. Batsmen were jealous of other batsmen who were scoring more runs than them. It was embarrassing. It was only when Vaughany took over and they got rid of the dead wood that the culture changed and we started winning. The only player from my early days with England I would have liked to have seen in the 2005 Ashes-winning team was Goughie. After that, nobody.

I always made a big effort to make any new players feel welcome in the dressing room. I was secure enough in myself to do that. I didn't see anyone as a threat, I saw them as a teammate first and foremost, someone I could help. Unfortunately, I got close to a couple of people, players I looked after when they first came into the team, who then dropped me when I needed their support. As soon as they had their feet under the table, they cosied up with the senior players and started knifing people. I'd sooner be open and get let down every now and again than closed all the time, but it's difficult.

But while sometimes the people you think will be there for you aren't, other times someone you didn't think you were particularly close to might surprise you. They might drop you a text or give you a ring out of the blue, and you'll think, 'Wow, that was nice.' Similarly, there were players I wasn't meant to get along with – according to sections of the press and the public – who I liked, such as Kevin Pietersen.

I never saw Kev as a major problem, I thought he was a straight shooter. If he had a beef with someone, he'd have it out with them. He became a problem in the England dressing room because of jealousy. He could be awkward and difficult, but he scored a lot of runs for England. And when he was scoring runs, he wasn't being awkward in the dressing room, because he was out in the middle. I appreciated Kev, because I could deal with him. Some people didn't, because they couldn't.

What I couldn't deal with was people making cheap digs behind other people's backs. That's why I've never written an autobiography that goes into great detail about my dealings with other people. If you don't have enough stories about yourself to fill a book, don't bother writing one. That's why it's called an autobiography, because it's about you. I might tell the odd funny tale about teammates or coaches or opponents, but I've seen so many autobiographies recently by former teammates (and coaches!) that just seem bitter and twisted. Your memoir shouldn't be about this or that person calling you nasty names in the dressing room, it should be more positive than that, surely? It reminded me of a piece of advice Duncan Fletcher once gave me: 'The weakest way to criticise someone is in print.' I thought, 'That's about right, well done, Duncan.' Then he slagged me off in his book!

It's good that you can get an instant response on social media, but if someone has a go at me, I just block them. I don't need that in my life. Who does? Actually, David Moyes. My mate, Big Bob from the social club, sent a letter to the *Lancashire Evening Post*, when Moyes was manager at Preston, saying what he thought was going wrong with the team and what could be done better. A few days after the letter was published, Big Bob got a knock on the door and when he answered it, Moyes was standing on his doorstep. He said, 'About that letter you sent to the paper, I'd be interested in a chat.' So Big Bob invited Moyes in, made him a brew and they sat down and had a deep and meaningful about football. Fair play to Moyes, but I couldn't be having that. Imagine me going round to some theatre critic's house, knocking on their door and saying, 'Hello, luvvy, I'm here about your review of my performance in *Fat Friends*. When you said I couldn't sing, I thought that was a bit uncharitable of you...'

Then there are the people who retweet and like compliments. What is wrong with you (Bear Grylls)? I've stopped following people (Bear Grylls) purely because they do that. These people will be absolutely cracking it, doing all these amazing things in their lives, why do they need to tell everyone what Carol in Luton thinks about their latest programme? It's pathetic. Matthew Syed and Robbie Savage retweet praise, and I hammer them for it on the podcast. Imagine walking down the street and shouting, 'I'm a legend! Look at me! People think I'm great!' That's basically what retweeting praise is.

I don't like praise, at least false praise, and I hate being patronised. Someone could be saying something really nice and I'll be thinking, 'You condescending bastard.' I'd sooner not be praised at all. And praise from me has got to be earned. If a woman has her hair done or buys a dress and it looks horrific, I'm not going to say I like it. How could you? You're not doing anyone a favour by doing that. And I can't congratulate mediocrity, as my kids are finding out. When my lad scored his first hundred for Lancashire, I praised him to high heaven, because he'd worked so hard to get there and I was so proud. But if either of them doesn't perform, I'll tell them they could have done better. It will be a constructive chat, but I don't think it's fair to tell them things are better than they are.

Social media has turned everyone into narcissists. Occasionally, I'll tweet something about my personal life and immediately think, 'Why have I done that?' Of the 1.4 million people who follow me on Twitter, I probably know about ten of them, if that.' Go on Facebook and it's just loads of people showing off about the great holiday they've been on, the big house they've bought, the expensive food they've eaten, or the wonderful family they've got. It's rubbing people's noses in it. Knobheads. They'll not post any pictures of the big row they've had or the meal they've eaten in complete silence because the bloke wet the bed the night before.

Another thing that bugs me about social media is when a famous person dies, everyone has to say their piece. You can't move for RIPs on Twitter. If you post something that isn't about that person's death, even if you never met them, someone will pipe up and say, 'Have you not seen the news? How could you be so insensitive?' or 'Why have you not said anything about such and such person dying?' I want to reply, 'Because I didn't know them, it's none of my business!' But they're just looking for a reaction, so I don't give them the satisfaction.

I hate myself for being on social media in the first place. I got my first mobile phone when I was 17, took it home and my dad said to me, 'They'll never catch on, you're wasting your money.' Now look at us. The first thing I do when I wake up in the morning is reach over, pick up my phone and check everything: text messages, emails, WhatsApp, Twitter. The irony is, I don't even want to be reached. I spend most of my time dodging calls. It's not that I'm a control freak, but I don't like not being in control, if that makes sense.

Imagine being a kid who grew up with all this technology. That's all they do all day, sit around looking at Snapchat and Instagram. It wouldn't surprise me if they suddenly announced that all this unseen technology we're surrounded by is frying our brains. It sometimes seems that way.

If mobile phones, televisions and computers had never been invented, everything would be better. I don't have much use for technology. If someone says, 'Do that on the computer', I struggle. But I don't need to know how, and I don't think most people do. I was sat watching the cricket with a mate and he had this app on his phone which tracked aeroplanes. Every time a plane went over, he'd tell me where in the world it had come from and where in the world it was going. Why would anyone want to know that? Why was he telling me this? People say the world is too complicated nowadays, but it's only complicated because people obsess over things that aren't important.

CHAPTER 15

WHAT HAVE YOU EVER DONE FOR ME?

Being let down

I don't like injustice; I hate it when people abuse their authority. When I was at school, I had a bit of a beef with this teacher, who gave me a detention for hitting a girl on the head with a ball in the yard. I said to him, 'I'm really sorry, but it was an accident. If I was that good at football that I could deliberately hit someone on the head from 50 yards away, I wouldn't be playing cricket. So I'm not having a detention for that.' The detention kept being put further and further back, and it ended up not happening.

A few weeks later I was playing in a pupils versus teachers football match. He had the ball and I smashed him from behind, hit him with arms and legs and everything, so that he was splattered all over the pitch. I'm a bit random at times, if I get something in my head and decide I'm going to do it, I'll do it. I was only 16, skinny, but still quite big. He got up and said, 'You got a problem, big man?' And I replied, 'No, sir, but it looks like you have.' He got right in my face and I thought we were going to have a fight, but he thought better of it and backed off. I wish I'd done that in the first year, because all the kids thought I was quite cool after that. Alas, I was leaving a week later.

I fell out with coaches and other authority figures quite a lot during my cricket career. Duncan Fletcher could really push my buttons, whether he knew it or not. In 2001, I played from May to September with a double hernia. Before the third Test against India, I turned up at Headingley with no kit, because I couldn't move and had no intention of playing. But they jabbed me up, sent me out there and I got two ducks and one wicket. I got picked for the Ashes tour that winter and during the first warm-up session I was walking around the ground, because I still couldn't run. Duncan Fletcher pulled me into his office and said, 'What are you doing?'

'I've got a double hernia, I can't run.'

'Yes, but when they said you can't run, I didn't think they meant you can't actually run...'

I was picked for the first Test in Brisbane, when Nasser Hussain won the toss, decided to bowl and the Aussies scored about 500. At one point, Matthew Hayden hit one up in the air, I was trotting after it in the outfield and missed it by a mile. Nasser threw his cap on the ground and sent me off the field.

I stayed on the tour, watching the boys getting hammered by every team we played. In Tasmania, they worked out I had something affecting an area in my body called the symphysis pubis. Above your willy is a hole in your pelvis, and they said they could inject it with painkiller. I thought, 'I've tried everything else, why not.' So I was laid on this bed with a towel over my meat and two veg, and in came this doctor and two nurses. The doctor pulled this massive needle out and I was thinking, 'Where the hell is he gonna put that?' By the time he'd removed the towel, it was less a meat and two veg and more a shiitake mushroom. He put the needle in and I let out this bloodcurdling scream. Even worse, my balls started disappearing, so that I looked like a Ken doll. I ended up saying to the nurses, 'It's usually bigger than this, but I'm really nervous...'

Eventually, Duncan pulled me into his office and gave me a bollocking for not being fit and committed to the cause. We had a team meeting straight afterwards and I had to wear sunglasses, because I'd been crying. Our relationship was never repaired. By all means bollock me for getting into trouble, but if you question my commitment to the team or my motives or my passion, that will really get to me. I always tried my best, you couldn't get any more out of me.

But usually I'd get into trouble because I was sticking up for someone else I thought was getting a hard time, especially younger players. Younger players would get hammered by older players who felt insecure about their place in the team, or get a rough time from a coach and feel like they couldn't speak up for themselves. So I'd speak up for them instead. I still do it now in the entertainment industry when I think people are taking liberties.

I've not got a problem with authority, I've got a problem with people abusing their authority. If I don't think authority is just, I'll question it or go against it completely. People get a title and automatically feel they deserve respect, but that's not the case. Leaders have to earn respect through their actions, their experience, their knowledge and achievements. Respect is not God-given.

There's nothing wrong with questioning authority, especially if you don't understand or agree with it. There's a time and place for it, and sometimes people do it for attention, to be noticed. Questioning authority in front of a group is not the best way to go about it, because you never want it to look like you're deliberately undermining someone. But if they can't answer the questions you ask or get upset, they're not very good leaders and shouldn't be in charge. If they can, fine, let's crack on. I don't mind being told.

I think I'd make a decent coach, because I've got no agenda. I'd be doing it for the right reasons, because all I'd want to do was make players better. If I thought I could offer that, I'd do it. But I felt that Duncan was very good at passing the blame. Don't get me wrong, I handed myself to him on a plate, but he was happy to tuck in.

After the pedalo incident, he summoned me to hotel reception. There were about 150 people there, including England fans and press, and he thought that was the right place to sack me as vice-captain. I wasn't that bothered about being sacked – I'd been captain and didn't like that either – it was the way he did it that bothered me. After he'd given me the news, he said, 'What have you ever done for me?'

I looked at him as if to say, 'What? I don't understand.'

'Andrew Strauss gets me trainers. Paul Collingwood gets me sunglasses. What have you ever got me?'

I was thinking, 'A big house in Cape Town and an OBE...'

I honestly thought he might be winding me up. I've got an ankle that is hanging off, my knees are knackered, and he's asking what I've ever done for him? What do I need to do to get back into his good books? Buy him a pair of Nike Air Max? Some Asics Gel? Does he want me to give him one off the wrist as well? I admit I was in a bad place emotionally, and I'm sure he'd deny it, but I remember it as if it was yesterday.

If I was playing well, Duncan would be all over me. If I wasn't, I was the root of all the evil, the reason England lost. I'd be thinking, 'Mate, I'm still trying my best.' I'd be lying if I said he didn't help me as a coach, but he also confused me. When I walked past him, I didn't know if he was going to speak to me or not. And he had a one-stop shop way of playing, which I couldn't do, so my batting got really mixed up. All I wanted to do was hit the ball as hard as possible. There's no two ways about it, I had a good run under him and the team had a good run under him. When I was giving my best performances for England, I was hardly speaking to him. But other people's experiences were very different. Marcus Trescothick, who was probably the best I ever played with, would talk about Duncan highly. In fact, if you spoke to everyone who played under Duncan, the response would be more positive than negative. So to say Duncan did nothing for England would be ridiculous. The record books show he was a very good England coach, maybe the best we've ever had.

Not long after the pedalo incident, we were having a training session in Barbados and everyone was called into a circle. Duncan wandered over and announced he was resigning. When Michael Vaughan said a few words, he started crying.

Paul Collingwood was trying his best to cry. Even Paul Nixon, who had been there five minutes, was trying to cry. I was thinking, 'Maybe I need to pinch my legs and put some chilli in my eyes, because I'm looking nowhere near upset enough.' What I actually did was look over at Steve Harmison and give him a look that said, 'Get in there, son!'

A lot of people retire with an axe to grind, and it's so sad to see people who had this great career, doing something they loved, and now all their energy is taken up with resentment towards a person or a former club or organisation. I was like that for a while, but it tires you out. Let it go, move on. So I don't bear a grudge against Duncan, because I don't actually think he ever meant to stitch me up. It was a weird relation-ship, but that was just what he was like, he was a natural deflector. We're never going to be pen pals, but I've given up not liking people.

In fact, I'd like to see Duncan again. I nearly did, when India were playing at Old Trafford a few years ago and he was their coach. I was in the nets with my boys, and I thought, 'Duncan's on the bus, brilliant.' I waited for about 45 minutes but he never got off. I really wanted to hug him and kiss him on the cheek. Partly to make him feel akward, but also to break the ice. It's not nice bearing grudges, especially against someone who you've shared so many wonderful memories with.

CHAPTER 16

BELLENDS ON BIKES

Health and fitness

The gym is a real cross-section of society, you've got people from all walks of life in there. But it can be an awkward place. There are people in the gym I like, Robbie Savage and a few other lads I train and have a coffee with, including old Eddie, who's 80. But I don't really want gym friends. You see someone for the first time and say hello, just to be polite. Second time, you speak a bit more. Third time, they've got you. I go to the gym to train, not to stand about talking to some bloke about the exercises he's doing on his pecs.

Someone will say, 'Do you mind spotting me?' I do, actually. I've got 45 minutes to do my work and get out of there, I've not got time to be putting your weights on for you. I don't want anyone commenting on my routine or complimenting me.

I know people say that men should say nice things to each other, and I might say the odd nice thing to a friend, but I don't want people sidling up to me in the gym and saying, 'You're looking in good nick, Fred, what's the secret?' They're probably only saying it in the hope that you'll say something nice back. But you are highly unlikely to find me saying, 'Oh, wow, you look fabulous.' That's not going to happen. They're my basic gym rules: don't have gym mates, don't give compliments, just train and then go home.

Then there are changing rooms and people wandering around naked. One day, I was doing my hair in the mirror, as I do nowadays, wearing just my pants. This man comes over, bollock naked, and says, 'All right, Fred?'

'Yeah, I'm all right.'

'You know my son...'

He started going on about his son, and what he was up to nowadays, and suddenly offered me a business card. I had no idea where he'd pulled this card from, so I said to him, 'Sorry, mate, I don't really know who you're talking about and I can't take that card, you did not have it in your hand just a second ago...'

There's this man who sits by the showers, cross-legged, with his balls resting on the bench. Nobody needs to see that. I took my lad in once when he was about six or seven. This naked man was reaching into his locker and my lad whacked him on the arse. My lad looked at me as if to say, 'How funny was that, Dad?' To be fair, it was quite funny, but not for this poor fella. He's got this little red hand print on his arse and when he turns around, he's got this confused look on his face, a mixture of anger and embarrassment, while you can also see him wondering whether he's allowed to have a go at somebody else's son. All I could do was shrug and say, 'Kids...'

I've cycled thousands of miles, but I have a love–hate relationship with cycling. I like some cyclists, but some of them are the biggest bellends you could ever hope to meet. They're just so righteous. You'll be driving along behind a cycling club, and they'll be riding two abreast. They're entitled to, but don't be a dick, you're holding everyone up! You get to within four feet of them when you overtake and they'll tell you you're too close. They go through red lights and think that's fine, or when they do stop at the lights, they'll do that silly thing where they balance without their feet on the ground, as if everyone in the queue is going to be impressed that a 50-year-old man can do such a thing. They go out and buy £10-grand bikes, essentially spending more money to make it easier. Some of these bikes have electric gears, presumably so their fingers don't get too tired. If you want to get fitter, get yourself a big steel bike with massive tyres! The bloke on a £10-grand bike is training less hard than the bloke on a bike that cost 200 quid. How does that make any sense?

I did a charity ride from Athens to London and encountered some of the worst people I've ever met. It was over five stages and it was a constant willy-waving contest. Who's got the most expensive bike? Who's got the lightest bike? Who's got the deepest-set wheels? Who looks like the biggest wanker in their branded fluorescent Lycra? They'd all have their Stradas out, comparing who had got up such and such hill the fastest. Unless you're the fastest in the world, don't bother showing me! There's probably been 200,000 people faster, and you're banging on about how fast you've gone? These people are wrong 'uns.

While I'm at it, what about personal trainers? They're the biggest robbery in the world. In my gym, you can pay £60 an hour for a personal trainer and all they do is stand around and watch you on a running machine or a bike or lifting weights. You can find out everything you need to know on the internet, all the machines have programmes on them, yet people get themselves a personal trainer and think they hold the key to life. And if you need someone to tell you to do something, don't do it. If I'm a boss of a business and I have to bring in a motivational speaker, I've failed at my job. You shouldn't have to rely on anyone else; rely on yourself. I like that Brian Clough quote: 'I believe in two things, Jesus Christ and me.'

You'll be out for dinner with someone, they'll order a burger and chips and say, 'I really shouldn't be eating this.' Too fucking right you shouldn't! Look at you! People talk about being big-boned. Big-boned? I've never seen a fat skeleton. If you take an X-ray of a small person and a big person, they'll look the same. We live in a society where everyone else is to blame. Everyone wants a quick fix. I've been fat and I've been skinny, so I know it's a very simple equation.

When I was fat and unfit, I was eating pizzas and drinking ten pints every night and not training. The strange thing was, I didn't realise. I remember turning up for an England fitness test and Dean Conway, the physio, put me on the scales and said, 'Bloody hell, Mongo (he used to call me Mongo, from *Blazing Saddles*), how did that happen? Last time I saw you, you were 14. Now you're 19 and a half.' I was getting dressed, looking in the mirror and thinking, 'You're looking all right there, Andrew...' Even when the England one-day team started playing in tight-fitting shirts, I didn't think I looked ridiculous. I look back at old pictures now and realise I very much did.

I tried all sorts of diets, including putting my fingers down my throat to make myself sick. For a while, I was doing that all the time, so that I was pretty much bulimic. I started doing it when I was out drinking and wanted to make a bit of room for a few more pints. Early in my England career, I got constant abuse about my weight. There was an article in one of the newspapers, with a picture of me on one side and Lennox Lewis, who was world heavyweight champion at the time and one of my heroes, on the other. It had this tale of the tape graphic, including the statistic: 'Lennox Lewis's reach – 84in; Andrew Flintoff's reach – For the pies'

That came out the same day as I was playing a one-day international at Old Trafford and I got absolutely hammered by the crowd. They'd call me all sorts, mainly 'fat bastard' but also Honey Monster. There would be grown men screaming at me, 'I want my honey!' It was just relentless.

When I had to lose weight fast on an England tour of India, making myself sick developed into a habit. I'd be sick in the toilet during lunch and go out and bowl for the rest of the day. I've been sick in grounds all over the world. But because I was losing weight, everyone was happy, so I cracked on. I'd gone from that fat fella who made his Test debut to getting into some kind of shape. A dietician came and gave us a talk, and she spoke about dealing with models, actors and athletes, mostly female, with eating disorders. I planned to pull her aside afterwards for a chat, until she said, 'But I can't imagine there's any of that going on with you lot.' At that moment I thought, 'Well, I can't say anything now.' I'd always thought of bulimia as something that affected women, and this dietician had just confirmed that suspicion.

I was always careful about it, made sure nobody was in the toilet when I was doing it. I thought I couldn't tell anyone, because I didn't want to show any signs of weakness. I wanted to come across as bulletproof. Rachael rumbled me on holiday in Dubai after we'd eaten in this restaurant with tiny portions. The meal cost a lot of money but it all ended up in the toilet before I'd even paid for it. As you can imagine, she was quite concerned. But once I'd told her, that was the first step on the road to stopping completely. As with just about everything I've done, I couldn't have done it without her. Eventually, I realised it wasn't healthy and that the only proper way to lose weight was through hard work and eating properly.

It would be nice if nobody gave a shit, but weight and appearance is such a big thing, especially in the TV world, and I don't think there's anything wrong with a bit of personal pride as long as it is healthy for them. People tell me I look in better shape now that when I played cricket. That's because I started training. I hated training when I was younger, saw it as a chore. Now it's become part of my everyday routine. It makes me feel better about myself.

I've been sucked in by the odd fad diet. When I stopped drinking, I started eating too much chocolate. You can buy one of those big Dairy Milks for a quid in Poundland, and I can get through two in a day. So I recently went on the C9 diet, which basically meant paying £120 for a box with hardly anything in it. There are powders and shakes and tablets, but you're effectively paying £120 not to eat for nine days. I mainly did it because my missus was on it, so I wasn't going to get cooked for. I'm not sure I even wanted to lose weight. I was just a bit bored, because I had nothing else on. That's how my mind works: 'What have I got on this week? Nothing? Right, I'll give that daft diet a go...'

CHAPTER 17

THE GAME'S GONE

The way things used to be

I don't feel sympathy for kids coming through today and the amount of scrutiny they're under – why would I feel sorry for someone who is embarking on a career as a professional sportsperson? But sport is getting very sterile and a bit boring because it's ultra-professional, ultra-technical and analysed to within an inch of its life. When I started playing for Lancashire, you finished the season in September, had the winter off, and turned up again the following April. Now, you're back in the nets in November and training all winter.

After losing my place in the England team in 2001, my management team hatched a plan to send me away for training with the academy. When I went to sign my contract, it said £20 grand on it. I said to John Abrahams, who I knew from Lancashire and who ran the academy, 'John, it says 20 grand here? Is that right?' John said, 'Oh, is that not enough?' I'd asked to come on the tour, and now they were paying me 20 grand. Happy days... until I found out we were going on a team-building exercise at Sandhurst Military Academy.

Team-building exercises aren't really my thing. Team-building exercises at military academies are about as far away from being my thing as you can possibly get. The first morning, we were being drilled in this sports hall, doing press-ups and sit-ups, and a few of the lads, including me, were struggling to keep up. This woman started screaming at one lad, so I piped up and said, 'He can't do it. He's trying. What's shouting at him going to achieve?' Then she started shouting at me, so I said, 'What's wrong? Why are you shouting at me? Please don't shout at me.' Then this bloke popped up and started shouting at me as well. As you've probably gathered, I don't like being shouted at.

All this pointless team-building stuff was followed by two days of survival. The plan was to dump us on the hills with our backpacks and survival kits, and we were supposed to find our way to different checkpoints and solve various puzzles. I was standing on a hill with Keysey, looking at what we had to eat, which turned out to be dried food and wasn't going to cut it. So I said, 'Tell you what, I'll nip to the shop.' I went to Sainsbury's, bought some crisps and chocolate bars, stuffed them in our bags and set off.

When I looked at the map, I realised we were just going round in a big circle, so I said, 'Lads, I'm making a decision here. Let's stash the bags in the bracken over there and we'll circle back and pick them up later.' So we stashed the bags, covered them up, and when we got to the first checkpoint this sergeant or whoever he was started shouting at us.

'Flintoff! Over here now! Where's your bag?'

'Well, I looked at the map, realised we were going in a big circle, and decided we'd stash them and pick them up when we circled back round.'

At this point, he got right in my face, so I could feel his spittle. 'Flintoff! The bergen is the most important part of a soldier's equipment!'

'I'll be honest with you, I didn't expect this reaction. I thought I was using my initiative. Why would I carry it if I don't have to? Seriously, it's heavy, and we've got a lot of walking to do...'

That wound him up even more. He told us to do this task, which involved some barrels and some pieces of wood, was miles easier than he said it was and we finished in a few minutes. Then I said, 'Is that it? What's next?' I couldn't help myself, but now he was wild. He stormed off, and half an hour later a couple of fellas appeared with a stretcher and a 100-kilogram dummy, which we had to carry for the next two days.

Because I read the map wrong, we ended up leaving the grounds and walking down this high street. People were tutting at us, saying stuff like, 'No wonder the country's in the state it's in, look at the state of these soldiers...' We got back on track and picked the backpacks up, but by the time we got back to the checkpoint it was dark, so we decided not to put the tents up and sleep under the stars instead. We were all sat around in a circle, emptying the crisps and chocolate onto a rug so that we're basically having a picnic, and this bloke came out of nowhere and started shouting at us. Again. He was kicking us in the back, standing on our fingers, booting the crisps and chocolate everywhere. Then he set us another challenge, which involved us trying to find a wagon in the dark and being hit over the head while we were doing it. The next day, after manoeuvres, we all had a dinner, and I got so drunk I had to be carried to bed by some soldiers, which was revenge for the 100-kilogram dummy.

In contrast, the academy trip to Australia was a bit of a jolly. The food was shocking, but because we were getting paid, we used to go to nice restaurants every night. I'd say to Keysey, 'Fancy an Italian? There's a lovely one in Adelaide.' And he'd rub his hands together and say, 'Yeah, Trev, let's 'ave some of that.' Then there was the Tuesday Night Club. There's this famous strip bar in Adelaide called the Crazy Horse, and we went there every Tuesday and got to know the staff very well. We'd all be in there, a bunch of academy lads who hadn't achieved anything in cricket yet, sipping champagne.

After the Christmas party, one of the blokes who ran the academy said, 'Lads, there's this place called the Crazy Horse I'd love to go to, would you like to join me?' As we were walking up the steps towards the entrance, he turned around and said, 'Have any of you lads been here before?' To which we all replied, 'No, mate, of course not...' But right on cue, this girl walked out and said to us, 'Gentlemen! Welcome back. Would you like your usual table? The champagne will be over in a minute...'

Because I was bowling quick, I got called up to play for England, so the lads sent me off with this massive night out. The following morning, I'd not packed my bags, and the manager, who was ex-army, was shouting at me to hurry up. So I thought, 'Fuck this', stuffed everything into my bags, slung them over my shoulders and walked out naked. This manager was going absolutely spare.

'Flintoff! What are you doing?'

'Going to India, to meet the lads...'

'Why aren't you wearing any clothes?'

'As long as I'm wearing a smile, that's all that counts...'

I fell in the car, flew to India, and that's when my England career started to take off.

The human element of sport is waning. When I started playing cricket, it wasn't very professional, but it was fun. At Old Trafford, there were two dressing rooms, one for the first team and one for the second team, and the second team dressing room doubled as the smoking room. Because Benson & Hedges sponsored the one-day tournament, there would be cartons of fags lying about all over the place. Even players who didn't smoke smoked. If players weren't playing, they were in the crowd watching. Or they'd be drinking with fans in the bar, and when the night was over, they'd walk out of Lord's and catch the Tube home. That was all normal. That's one of the reasons darts is so successful, because it's one of the few sports where the crowd can identify with the players. They look at these big fellas on stage and think, 'These are just normal lads, who like a pint and a punt in the bookies.'

Cricket has gone the other way. When I started, a team photograph consisted of the team, the coach and the manager. By the time I finished, there were dieticians, shrinks, bag-carriers, social media gurus, someone to pick your nose and scratch your bum. I'm surprised there was a camera lens wide enough to fit us all in. I can vividly remember Alastair Cook turning up for the first time, taking his top off in the dressing room and looking like someone off a Calvin Klein advert. All of a sudden, people were drinking protein shakes after a day's play, instead of four or five pints. They didn't drink coffee or tea, they were having electrolyte drinks instead. I used to come off for lunch excited, because I ate what I wanted. I didn't want pasta and dry chicken, I wanted a curry. Give me a big pile of fish and chips and I'll play better in the afternoon, because I'll be happy. Give me pasta and I'll have the hump.

At the start of my career, I ate everything. Me and Paddy lived near a takeaway place called By the Slice, which served pizza the size of bin lids. We had one of those almost every night, because it was easy. Life with Paddy was lively. We would be chasing nights out here, there and everywhere, go out until whatever time, get up the next morning, train half the day and go back out. That was our week, every week, and we wondered why the training wasn't having any effect. We'd have had to run a marathon every day to lose any weight.

We didn't do any housework, we had cleaners in to do that, although a forensics team might have been more appropriate. We didn't really have a clue about grown-up life. We went to Bodrum, Turkey, on an 18–30 holiday, got sold a dummy by the travel agents, who told us it was packed all year round. When I finally turned up – two days late, because I forgot my passport – there was nobody there. But when you're that age, everything just seems funny.

But I wouldn't change a thing, because you've got to live life while you're young. You're not going to be able to eat pizza every night when you're 65. There were times during my career when I thought, 'I should have worked harder, I should have done my homework, I shouldn't have had that night out, I should have done this and done that.' I found myself wearing shirts with 'XXXX' on the tag. Back then I was too big even for Jacamo.

As a result, I'd turn up for games not knowing how it was going to go. I could nearly handle getting beaten if I'd done everything I could, I couldn't handle it if I hadn't. But there's no point dwelling on it. People want me to regret it, and regret it on my behalf, but I don't. I loved it, and I think I ended up doing all right on the pitch. I played plenty of games for England, more than I might have done, given the injuries and pain I was playing through.

Whenever I got into a scrape, the first person I thought of was my mum and her embarrassment. But apart from not inviting my mum and dad to Buckingham Palace, the only thing I'd change is every shot I played when I got out. I can never understand it when people say, 'What would you have done differently?' It doesn't make sense to me, because when you make a decision, however that decision looks in hindsight, you thought that was the right decision to make based on your state of mind and circumstances at that time.

Regrets are absurd, because you're not the same person who made the decision you're supposed to be regretful about. Also, everything I've done has made me the person I am today. I'm not saying I'm perfect and wouldn't change anything, but it's all part of the great tapestry of life. What's the point in sitting around and thinking, 'I wish I hadn't gone on that pedalo or got clattered at 10 Downing Street'? Or 'I wish I'd brought Duncan Fletcher an apple every day'? Seriously, I was pissed trying to get on a boat. Who cares? I didn't kill anyone, I was just having a bit of a giggle. And it wasn't the night before a game, it was two nights before a game. And the game was against Canada! I could have done it during the game...

And it was that sort of stuff that got me work after I retired from cricket. Can you imagine Jonny Wilkinson on *A League of their Own*? I'm not criticising Jonny, he was the perfect professional and I'm sure he's doing very well for himself, but that's why I've got some of the gigs I have – because I wasn't the perfect professional. Sometimes you do things that seem ridiculous but turn out for the best. Like that time I punched a wall in the dressing room and had two pins inserted in my hand. I had eight weeks off and got picked for an England tour. It was one of the best things I ever did.

Number 10 was just a bit of fun, and I wouldn't change a thing about it, because I didn't want to meet Tony Blair anyway.

It was his government that hung us out to dry during the World Cup in Zimbabwe, when we had to forfeit a game because they were worried that Robert Mugabe might turn up and try to shake our hands. When I got hammered, I'd get something in my head and be even more stubborn than normal, so when one of Blair's aides asked if I'd like to meet him, I decided to sit on a swing in the garden and have a beer with Harmy instead.

As an aside, I was at Number 10 recently and Theresa May did this speech. Her opening gambit was, 'Against our better judgement, we've allowed Freddie Flintoff back.' I nearly shouted out, 'Look, Theresa, David Cameron used the same line when I was here last time.'

Afterwards, I bumped into her on the steps and she said, 'I hope you were all right with that?'

'No, I was offended actually.'

'Oh. I am sorry.'

'Only joking!'

Poor woman is trying to keep the country from falling apart and she's got some smart alec former cricketer giving her lip. That's all she needs.

If I was playing cricket now, I think I would have had to conform. It's not that I didn't conform, I just liked to do certain things my own way. I like to think I would have still been my own man – if that's at all compatible with conforming – but it's a different world now. The kids all come through academies together and are taught to behave, as well as play, in the same way.

Now, everyone is so guarded. Even I have to be guarded. Once I get going, I'm not sure what's going to come out of my mouth, but I am also very aware that when I speak at functions I have to be careful what I say, because people will be filming on their phones. If I say one word out of place or make a joke about the wrong person, it could be all over the internet the next day.

Women's sport is a tricky one, a subject that is fraught with danger. Men's cricket has been going for over a hundred years and is constantly improving, so that it's probably the best it's been. The women's game is a lot newer and not fully professional yet. It would be great if more people were willing to invest in it, especially at grass-roots level, but as it stands the crowds are smaller, the TV viewing figures are smaller, it doesn't bring in as much sponsorship. The same can be said for women's football and women's rugby.

I think we should celebrate women's cricket for what it is. Forget about the men and what they're earning. They're different games, at different stages in their evolution.

Women's cricket is making great strides, and of course there is so much room for improvement. The women's game shouldn't be patronised – someone needs to grab hold of it, give it a shake, and make changes. The alternative is me saying everything is fine, which is tantamount to suggesting that's all women are capable of.

But it's a conundrum: improvements can only be made if people are willing to invest in it at grass-roots level, and only when those improvements are made will people watch it in the same numbers as they watch men's cricket.

I don't see why an eight-year-old girl shouldn't start playing with an eight-year-old boy and for them both to come through the ranks together. If she's good enough, good luck to her; if she's not, at least she might get better faster. It certainly makes sense to have female batsmen practising against male bowlers. And if the batters improved, then the bowlers would have to get better in order to compete. That might be the only way of finding women bowlers who can send it down at 80mph, instead of 70mph, which is barely medium pace in men's cricket.

One of the reasons I like Geoffrey Boycott is that he says what he thinks. I know people have got beefs with him and he's stiffed a lot of people, but he'll tell me to my face what he says on the telly or the radio. Despite all the waffle, I respect him as a player and a person. He likes to be the centre of it all, but that's why he's such a good pundit, because he calls it like he sees it, and sometimes that can be brutal. More importantly, he wants people to do well and he wants England to do well.

When I first started playing for England, he wouldn't call me by my name. He'd be on commentary and say, in that thick Yorkshire accent of his, 'Here he is, that big lad from Lancashire. He's rubbish...' Because he thought I was crap, he didn't think I deserved to be called by my name. I only really got to know him through my wife Rachael. Because of her work, she had to go to the cricket every now and again, and one day she didn't have any internet connection where she was. So she went to the media centre, got chatting to Geoffrey and it was only because of that that he started talking to me. From that day on, he started calling me by my name on telly. I was no longer the big, rubbish lad from Lancashire.

But even when I see him now, he still hammers me. I took the boys to Lord's and showed them round the media centre. I was randomly opening doors, and we met Bumble and Shane Warne and Brett Lee, before Geoffrey invited us into his commentary box. I said to the kids, 'This is Geoffrey', and Geoffrey was off: 'I like your dad, lads, but I love your mum...'

Bit weird...

'Your dad could bowl a bit, but batting? Useless. He were thick! Careless!'

A few days earlier, I'd shown the boys a clip of Geoffrey hitting a spectator with a bat, so my youngest said, 'Are you the fella who hit the man with your bat?' Geoffrey was all flustered – 'What? What?' – but I like characters, it's people like Geoffrey who keep the game interesting.

You sit and listen to the stories nowadays and think, 'Come on, you've not got a clue lads, not got a clue...' It's a different world. Everyone will be sat there on their phones, texting and posting pictures on Instagram. But I blame hair straighteners the most. When I first saw Paul Collingwood straightening his hair in the dressing room, I knew the game was gone. How can you expect someone to play through a bit of pain when they're worried about split ends? I hung in there for a while, but towards the end of my cricket career, I was looking around the dressing room and thinking, 'I don't really know anyone any more, all my mates have gone.' The culture was different, the language was different, what was and wasn't acceptable was different.

I was in the dressing room towards the end of my career and someone walked in with new hair. One day he was half-bald, the next he had this thatch on his head. I was sat there thinking, 'This is a gift, an open goal, I'm having this', but nobody else was saying anything. I couldn't understand it. Eventually I said, 'All right mate, how's your hair?', and my teammate appeared behind me and started making the cutthroat gesture. I felt bad and ended up having a 20-minute discussion about the merits of hair transplants. I was confused. Why was everyone suddenly being so nice to each other?

CHAPTER 18

WATERSTONES, NOT WETHERSPOONS

Battling the booze

When someone gives up booze, you often hear people say, 'He's not the same person any more.' They're right, I'm not. When you're four or five pints in, you are a different person, it alters your personality. I was more fun when I drank, the life and soul of the party. But I was bored of being that person. People tell me I've become boring, and it's true. I've had to be quite ruthless, cut ties with people I used to drink with. And because I don't go to the pub any more, the gym has become my night out. As sad as it might sound, I spend the whole time at the gym laughing with Robbie.

My mate Paddy – who was my best man and is godfather to my daughter – calls me boring all the time. It's fine, because he's bang on. I'm quieter, more introverted. But, jokes aside,

Paddy accepts me for who I am. I take it as a weird kind of compliment, because it means I'm finally happy being me. All those years, being the life and soul of the party in pubs and bars across the land, and that person was just a version of myself brought on by alcohol.

When I started playing cricket, drinking was normal for a county player. I might drink seven, eight, nine pints a day. You'd walk off the field and the 12th man would take an order. You'd have a couple in the dressing room, a couple with the opposition in the bar, a couple with dinner and a couple more after dinner.

As terrible as it might sound, drinking bolstered my confidence and helped me gain acceptance. At the same time, because I wanted to be seen as different – and whatever I lacked in ability I wanted to make up with bravado – I'd sometimes drink when other people didn't and not drink when others did. I'd go out, score runs the next day and people would be saying, 'Bloody hell, how did he do that? He didn't even sleep last night.' And I'd be thinking, 'Actually, I was in bed before you.' A lot of it was an act, part of the mystique.

A lot of how I behaved as a cricketer was about maintaining that mystique. During the final Test of the 2005 Ashes series, me and the missus had dinner with Neil Fairbrother and his wife. We drank a few bottles of red and the following morning

I decided to turn up to the Oval early. When the Aussies got off the team bus, I was standing outside having a cigarette, bidding them all a cheery good morning. Once I'd finished my fag, I ran upstairs and positioned myself in the corridor, so that they had to pass me again as they made their way to the dressing room. I was standing there saying, 'Morning, lads! Lovely day!' and they were looking at me as if I was mad.

When I went out to warm up, Glenn McGrath and Brett Lee were bowling to the wicketkeeper Adam Gilchrist. So I got a ball out of our bag, wandered over and said, 'Lads, my boys are all playing football and messing about, do you mind if I join in with you?' They looked at each other as if to say, 'What's this lad on?' before Glenn said, 'Yeah, mate, if you like.' I marked out my run-up, came hurtling in, pinged one through to Gilchrist, he took it above his head, threw the ball back and I said, 'Cheers, that'll do me.' As I was wandering off, Glenn said to me, 'Mate, do you ever get stiff?' I replied, 'Stiff? Never heard of it...' When I got back to the dressing room, I collapsed in a heap, because I was as stiff as a board. Then I went out and bowled them out.

A couple of times I did get the dosage wrong, gambled on the weather being bad and woke up in the morning to be greeted by bright sunshine. The night before I scored a hundred against South Africa at Lord's in 2003, the knock which turned my career around, I was hammered. That was Michael Vaughan's first game as Test captain, so he was slightly on edge. He was even more on edge after we got an absolute battering over the first few days.

After day three, Vaughany popped into the hotel bar on his way out for dinner with his missus, saw me and Harmy and said, 'What are you two doing?' We said, 'Having a couple of pints and heading to bed.' One pint quickly turned into three, and when Vaughany returned at about 1 a.m., me and Harmy were still there. As he was probably within his rights to do, Vaughany tried to give me a bollocking.

'Mate, what are you doing? You're battered!'

'Don't worry about me. I bet you I'll score a hundred tomorrow.'

'You won't.'

'Okay, let's put some cash on it.'

'How much?'

The following morning, I was sat on the window ledge on the balcony, feeling awful. Jimmy Anderson said, 'You all right?' To which I replied, 'Mate, I'm hanging out of my arse. But I've got to score some runs, because I've had a bet with Vaughany and he knows I was pissed last night. If I don't, I'm for it.'

It was a dead game by that stage, but I went out, played some shots and entertained the crowd. I reached my hundred in no time, and when I came off, Vaughany had a big grin on his face. We still lost the game by a landslide, but in his post-match interview, Vaughany said I'd spared some embarrassment for the team and clawed back a bit of respectability, which was nice. The one downside was he didn't honour the bet.

That was one time drinking ended well, although a few times it went badly. On an A-team tour of Zimbabwe, we ended up in this rough nightclub in Bulawayo. These rugby lads were having a pyjama party, and when one of them squared up to me in only his pants, I pulled them down and ran off, flicking Vs. He swung a punch, I slipped it – using my very proficient boxing skills – and Steve Harmison, who was dancing on a stool, was taken out instead. Harmy popped up off the floor, swung at this lad, missed, and hit Vaughany flush on the chin. Now Vaughany's on the deck and the whole thing is like a slapstick comedy. I looked around at the backup, saw Vikram Solanki, Darren Maddy and Chris Read, our little wicket-keeper, and thought, 'Shit.'

Suddenly, this rugby team has evacuated the building and a bouncer has tapped me on the shoulder and said, 'You need to take this outside.' I was thinking, 'We've got nothing to take outside.' When we got outside, there was this big pit, like something from *Braveheart*, and this rugby team were lined up on one side and we were lined up on the other. I walked to the middle to discuss an armistice, explained that there had been a terrible misunderstanding, and Harmy came flying over the top, arms and legs swinging, before the police turned up and bundled us into the back of a van.

But if I hadn't drunk, I don't reckon I would have been the player I was. Some people say I might have been better, but who really knows? Drinking was just part of my personality, as a person and as a cricketer. Maybe it was why I sometimes failed, maybe it was why I sometimes succeeded. It got me into trouble occasionally, but it also did me a lot of favours.

Drinking meant escaping, getting away from what was going on in my head. I never did drugs, even though they were rife at school. I've got an issue with drugs for the obvious reasons, but also because I struggle with the idea of shoving something up my nose which has been chopped up in the jungle and stuffed up someone's arse for the trip over to England. I might as well go around sniffing arses. And cocaine turns people into complete bellends. I struggle with wittering at the best of times; talking to someone on cocaine could make my head explode.

Some people take drugs, some people play golf, some people potter around the garden. I liked to drink. That was my hobby, just like chess was my hobby when I was a kid. I still play a bit of chess, although my latest thing is online Scrabble. I scored a

96 the other day, for 'quiz', on a triple letter. And did you know 'zo' and 'qin' were words? I'm really into it at the moment, but I'll get bored of it soon and stop. That's what happened with the drink. I got to the point where I thought, 'This is not doing it for me any more.'

I looked at all the things I'd been doing that involved drinking and realised I didn't enjoy any of them. I'd go to a function or dinner to have a drink. I'd play golf to drink on the course. Eventually I realised that drinking was just my way of getting through things. And if the drinking was the only part I liked, why not just sit on my own and drink? And when you start doing that, you're in serious trouble.

Drinking started catching up with me the next day. I'd get terrible hangovers that would make my mind feel ten times worse than normal. I used to be good at drinking, but not any more. I'd be getting slaughtered and passing out in bars, or making a dick of myself. I'd be waking up cringing about what I might or might not have done the night before. And as you get older, you get more and more feary. I got fed up of feeling like that, tired of my reputation. People would revel in telling me the stupid things I'd done. There should be a rule against that – whatever happened on a night out while drunk should never be mentioned again. But I'd be sat there in the morning, trying to piece the night before back together again, and someone would pipe up and say, 'Oooh, what about you last night?' Shut up! Shut up! Oh, God...

I'd still have an occasional great night with my mates, but most of the time the drinking was masking the fact I was in a situation I didn't really want to be in. I've got so many happy memories from drinking, but I started to get too many bad ones – or not, if you know what I mean.

When I finally knocked it on the head a few years back, it was difficult for the first week or so, because it felt like I was left with nothing. But I slowly got used to it. I miss it every now and again, but not enough to want to start again. The best thing about giving up drinking is getting up in the morning and taking the kids to school without a screaming headache. Unfortunately, I haven't been able to shake off the reputation.

That happens in life, people get labelled for all time for things they did a long time ago, even when they've tried very hard to change. When Matthew Syed brought out one of his books, I went to Waterstones at about 9 a.m. before it was open, knocked on the door, and this lad opened up, stuck his head around the door and said, 'Are you sure you're in the right place? This is Waterstones, not Wetherspoons...' Funny bastard.

From that moment I got involved in the Guinness drinking game in Guernsey, I was in the thick of everything. Drink gave me confidence, opened doors, made me feel welcome. So

I'm not one of those people who's going to start saying, 'Oh, drinking is terrible, a scourge, destroyed my life, I'm so much better without it.' I vowed never to be one of those people who takes pride in telling you they no longer drink. You know the type – you'll be at the bar, ask them what they want and they'll reply, 'Oh, I've given up.' So what? Just tell me you want a Coke or a glass of water, stop being so smug and pompous about it. I've never heard anyone say, 'No thanks, I'm a complete dick when I drink. You wouldn't want to see me drunk, best just get me a lemonade'.

Life isn't necessarily better without drink – that's why people drink! They drink for the same reason they take drugs or drive cars fast, because they get this enormous buzz out of it. For me, drinking was mostly good. It gave me some of my best times and did me a lot of favours. But it evolved into a love–hate relationship. I couldn't control it any more, I had a problem with it, it became an issue. I'm not some kind of hero for giving drink up, it's just that I was rubbish at it. What's heroic about that? Now, I don't have a relationship with drink at all. I guess you could say that me and the drink are divorced.

CHAPTER 19

GOAT KILLER

The call of the wild

While my social horizons have broadened since I retired from cricket, one thing I haven't become is more cultured. It annoys me, culture. Or at least the word does. What is culture? I struggle with it, to be honest. Culture seems to be things that other people tell you that you should like. I don't like being told what I should watch or read or listen to, I want to make my own mind up.

I've got an artistic streak. I'm quite creative, enjoy colouring in. I like some art, but some of it is just rubbish. I was in an art gallery the other day and there was a blob on a canvas, and a frame on a wall with nothing in it. What's that all about? I was in a restaurant recently and there was a cow in a tank. That's not art, that's a dead cow in a tank. I like reading, but I like reading what I want to read. I've read all of Ben Elton's books, all of Irvine Welsh's books, and my favourite book of all is *To*

Kill a Mockingbird. I tried to read Harper Lee's second one, which came out more than 50 years later, but got five pages in and gave up. She should have quit while she was ahead.

I went to France recently, performed in cabaret with Jamie Redknapp at the Lido for *A League of Their Own*. I thought, 'I'm in Paris, I'm not just gonna sit in a restaurant with Jamie all day, I'll do some exploring.' So I went for a walk around Notre-Dame Cathedral and was completely blown away, but not by what you'd expect. Don't get me wrong, the cathedral was nice, but it was the walls of the Seine that I couldn't get my head around. I just found myself looking at these massive walls for ages, thinking, 'Why is everyone taking pictures of the cathedral? Look at the walls on this river! They're massive!'

I'm convinced that a lot of the time, people don't see the same things as each other. Someone will say to me, 'Look at that, it's brilliant', and I'll be thinking, 'No, it's not, it's shit.' But I'll be fascinated by things that other people don't even notice. When I drove from Monaco to Milan, I couldn't believe the tunnels. I was more amazed by those tunnels than I was by Victoria Falls or the Taj Mahal. I love tunnels, there's a mystery about them. Them and bridges. How on earth do they do it? They're talking about digging a tunnel through the Pennines, from Manchester to Sheffield. What a complete waste of time and money. Who needs to get to Sheffield quicker? Who needs to get to Sheffield at all?

To me, culture is more about different people than buildings or books. And the best thing about doing TV is not the money it brings in, but the life experiences. I basically come up with things I want to do and see if someone wants to pay me to do it. Like going around Britain in a chip van. I wanted to do a travelogue-type show, I liked fish and chips, asked Sky if they thought it was a good idea, and they said yes. Sometimes I'll come up with an idea, pitch it at a meeting, they'll give it the thumbs-up, and I'll walk away almost giggling, because I can't quite believe it. Pitch youth hostelling with Chris Eubank to enough people and eventually someone will say yes. I guarantee you.

I met Rob Penn while I was making the fish and chip show. He's a green crusader, as well as a keen cyclist, so we did a do-gooder show together, which involved us riding and camping along 1,000 miles of the Amazon, trying to save trees. And a few years ago, I did a series for the Discovery Channel, *Freddie Flintoff Goes Wild*, which involved me being dropped into the middle of nowhere in various far-flung places and basically seeing if I'd die or not.

I spent ten days with the Masai in Africa, walking through Tanzania. We flew in, drove for hours and met this bloke Thomas, who was dressed in all his robes. The first day I got there, they tried to teach me to fight with sticks and throw a spear, in case we got attacked by a lion. The plan was to meet up with a wildebeest migration, so we were walking about 20 miles a day, in burning heat, with a big backpack on. Not for the first time I thought, 'I'm in the wrong job.'

The elders wanted to have a welcome feast, which they put on in this little hut. They picked out a goat, which was led into the hut, and Thomas said, 'You've got to kill it.'

'I can't kill a goat. I'm no goat killer. Why would I want to kill a goat?'

Thomas kept on at me, and eventually I said, 'Go on then, give me the knife...'

'No, you don't cut its throat, we want to keep the blood. You've got to strangle it.'

'I'm not strangling a goat!'

'Okay, so you'll have to suffocate it...'

So I was in this hut, rolling about on the floor with a goat, my hand over its mouth and nostrils, and its bleating was getting more and more subdued. When it finally expired, Thomas and his mates cracked open its belly, stuck their hands in and started lapping up the blood.

Suddenly Thomas said, 'You've got to have some blood.'

'I don't want any blood.'

'You've got to, otherwise you'll upset the others.'

I wasn't really worried about drinking the blood, I was worried about where their hands had all been. Put it this way, I couldn't see any rolls of Andrex, and there was no sign of any antiseptic soap. So I was drinking this blood, smacking my lips as if I was absolutely loving it, even though it was disgusting, and all the time thinking, 'I cannot wait to tell people back home about this...'

We carried on walking for a couple of days. There were Masai running past us the whole time, and we bumped into one of Thomas's mates. This fella looked confused and said to Thomas, 'Is he skint?'

'I don't think so. Why?'

'So why is he walking in this heat? Tell him to hire a car.'

We arrived at this boma, which is a little group of houses with an animal pen in the middle. We got inside this hut, and it was pitch black. They gave me a bowl of ugali, which is like a rice porridge that you eat with your hands, and as I was eating it, this woman came out of nowhere and sat next to Thomas. I was looking at Thomas as if to say, 'You all right there, mate?' And he was looking at me with this smile on his face, as if to say, 'She's for you.' So I told him that he'd have to tell her that nothing is going to happen, romance-wise.

Later, I was next to the fire, trying to sleep, and there was all this smoke going in my face. Thomas was snoring next to me, so I went outside and slept with the dogs. When I woke up in the morning, I had conjunctivitis and my eyes were in agony. We set off walking again, and by the following night, word had got round that there was a white man walking. We arrived at this village, were met by these tribal elders who had laid on this meat feast. Alas, it wasn't a meat feast from Pizza Hut (I can only imagine the Serengeti branch had recently closed), it was just piles and piles of unidentifiable meat and this horrible soup.

I was sat there with all these fellas in their robes, trying to get down this soup that's making me feel sick, and suddenly they all decided to go to bed. I said, 'What, here? Just on the ground?' So I was lying on the dirt, with a blanket over me, and it suddenly dawned on me that Thomas was spooning me. I knew Thomas quite well by this point, so I just gave him a nudge, told him to get off and went back to sleep. When I opened my eyes, I saw a cat walking towards me and a spear over my shoulder. It was Thomas's mate, and he was whispering in my ear to stay still. I thought it was a leopard – I wanted it to be a leopard – but it turned out it was just a civet, which is about the size of a domestic cat, and Thomas's mate was being dramatic.

The next day, we came across this village full of kids. I had my iPad with me, which had Tetris and this card game on it.

The kids got properly into it and were challenging my high score in no time. When they saw themselves on my camera, they thought I'd captured their spirits. And I couldn't help thinking, 'My God, I think I've destroyed the Masai culture in a few hours...'

In Australia, I spent ten days in the bush with this Aborigine bloke, his missus and their kid. He took us crocodile hunting, and our boat nearly got flipped over. He threw a spear at the crocodile and told me to jump in and drag him out of the water. I declined. This fella's heart wasn't really in it. The first night we were there, we stayed in a lodge in the middle of Arnhem Land, which we had to get special permission to be in. The plan was to roam from the lodge and camp out in the bush, but this fella just returned to the lodge every night so he could have a few drinks and sleep in a proper bed.

One night, me and Mungo, my cameraman-director, slept in a cave on our own. Another night, we slept next to a river. It was awful. The only time our guide spoke was when he asked for a gun to shoot some fruit bats, which he then served up for dinner.

In Borneo, we searched for pygmy elephants in the jungle. The big problem was, I'm pretty sure our guide, this fella called Eric, was an absolute chancer. His story was that he'd rescued a baby elephant from a river and returned it to his mum, and the herd was eternally grateful. As we were walking, Eric kept saying, 'We will find them, because they know me, they like me and never forget.' When we finally tracked them down, they charged us. I was thinking, 'Eric, I thought you were meant to be good pals with this lot?'

When I went to Botswana, I filmed it myself. I flew in, took another aeroplane five hours into the bush, spent another hour in a helicopter and was finally dropped off at the camp. I was taught survival techniques for three days, then got dumped somewhere else, with a list of coordinates in my backpack. I didn't really listen to the survival lessons, which was a bit daft, because all I had to live off for a week was a cup of rice. I was armed with a machete and an air horn, but my biggest friends were a big bag of tobacco and some Rizlas. If I wasn't going to eat, I'd smoke every plant I could instead.

First night, I ate all the rice. I was meant to boil my water, but it took too long, so I drank it straight from the river. Second night, I was going to get rid of my tent and sleep rough, but it started bucketing down. I could hear hyenas and lions and all sorts, and the hyenas kept getting closer, so every second day I had to move. But I didn't follow the coordinates, so didn't know where I was.

Because I love animals, I pitched my tent by a watering hole. Nothing turned up, I got a bit bored, so I went and climbed some trees. From up there, I could see zebras and giraffes and, off in the distance, elephants. It was only when I returned to civilisation that I was told that someone had been tracking me and I'd had a close encounter with a lion. The tracker said to me, 'You did well there, climbing that tree when the lion walked behind you.' I said, 'I didn't see any lions, I was just climbing trees...' Up until then, this tracker must have thought I was the lovechild of a Masai warrior and David Attenborough.

While I was walking towards these elephants, I stepped on a termite mound. I was filming this herd while all these termites were biting my legs, when an elephant appeared from behind a tree, about 20 feet away. When it started flapping its ears, waving its trunk about and making these weird noises, I thought it was trying to shoo away flies. But later on, the tracker said, 'Well done on reading that elephant.' I thought, 'Mate, I had no idea, I thought he was annoyed because he had a swarm of flies buzzing around his head.'

The penultimate night, I could feel the atmosphere change. The insects were making a racket, the animals were shouting and screaming, and I suddenly heard these booming sounds, which I realised was lions approaching. I'd been told that if I built a massive fire, the lions wouldn't come near me. So I built this fire, set two cameras up facing in opposite directions, got in my tent and settled in for the night. When I watched the footage back, there were lions prowling in front of the cameras. Imagine the headlines: 'Flintoff Eaten by Lions'. Mind you, it's better than 'Hard, Fast and Short of a Length'.

When I get home from being on one of these adventures, I'll drop things into the conversation – 'There was a lion outside my tent' – and Rachael will say something like, 'Oh, nice. Cup of tea?' What does she think of my life? Probably not much, but it's better that way, it keeps you grounded.

The conversations I have with my mum and dad are weird. My mum will say, 'What you been up to?'

'Me and Jamie were performing in cabaret at the Lido in Paris.'

'Oh, nice. What have you got on next?'

'Me and Jamie are taking penalties in the San Siro in Milan.'

'Oh, nice...'

I'd like to share the experiences I've had with my friends and family but I'm scared of sounding like a dick. It sounds like I'm bragging, but it's just my life, weird as it is.

CHAPTER 20

STRIKING A BALANCE

Family comes first

There have been times when I haven't got my work–life balance right, especially recently. But I'm not the only one. Most people don't have a choice, they just work as hard as they can to provide for their families. For them, it's not about buying luxuries or going on extravagant holidays, it's about putting food on the table and paying for gas, electricity and the mortgage. They wish they could watch their kids play football on a Saturday morning or pick them up from school instead of going to work, but I'm more fortunate than that, because I have more choice.

In the last year or so, I've taken far too much work on, stuff I don't really need to do. And now I'm entering middle age, I can tell when I'm working too hard, because I get tired like I never used to. It's the fear of missing out on something, of not taking a job that might lead to another one, or not meeting someone who might enable me to do something I'd really like to do. It's taken me a while to understand that I'd sooner miss out on the odd job than miss out on what my kids are doing. My kids might say I still don't understand it completely. But the plan was always to get myself into a position where I can pick and choose a little bit more, which will hopefully happen soon.

I knew this passage would be challenging, that I'd chuck myself into loads of things, some of it would hit the spot and some of it wouldn't. There are times when I think, 'I could do without this at the moment', especially when I'm chasing my tail here, there and everywhere. Ironically, because I take on too much, I end up saying no to everyone. I swerve it for a day, another day passes, and then I think, 'Hmmm, is it too late to reply now?' The worst is when someone sends you a message on WhatsApp and they can see when you've read it from the blue tick. Why would anyone invent something like that? And then people will get pissed off when you turn the notifications off. It bothers me that I can't physically do what everyone wants me to do. But in the end, I hope I'll have a clearer idea of what direction I want to go in.

It's been a steep learning curve, especially from a presenting and acting point of view. I've got some good commercial deals, done some good TV, but I've also done some turkeys. It's hard when you're doing something you know is crap, and there are a few shows I've done that I look back on and cringe a bit.

I've sold things in the past and thought, 'Why would anyone want this?' I sold petrol once, for a 50p weekly reduction. I was in the back of a car, explaining to this journalist why it was such a special deal, thinking, 'There must be more to life than this...' I speak at the odd corporate do, but I've got a price, because I did one a few years ago which was absolutely awful, one of the worst experiences of my life.

I'd just kicked off a stand-up tour and the opening night in Preston had gone great. It was a home crowd and I killed it. This corporate do was at Lord's, only about 70 people, and I was thinking, 'This will be a piece of piss, they're obviously cricket people, why else would they be at Lord's?' The plan was to shorten the routine I'd done the night before but, as a wise man once said, no plan survives first contact with the enemy.

Before I got changed, I had a bath in the away dressing room, and while there, a tour group came through and started taking photos. I thought, 'Perfect, I'll open up with that, embellish it a bit, crack on.' But it turned out the do was for a manufacturing company, and I quickly realised there was absolutely no crossover between their worlds and mine. I did the story about the bath, not a murmur. I hit them with one of my bankers early, not a peep. There was a function next door in the Long

Room, and there were all these ex-players standing at the window making faces at me, knowing I was dying on my feet. I could feel sweat running down my back, soaking my shirt, and because I was now panicking about sweating, I was sweating even more.

I tried more funny, didn't work. I tried sincere, didn't work. I tried factual, didn't work either. Literally, no one was interested. I opened it up to the floor for questions, not one. All they were here for was the free food and drink, I was just an inconvenience for half an hour. I vowed never to do another corporate do until someone made me an offer I couldn't refuse. To borrow an expression from Jamie Redknapp, who probably borrowed it from his dad, just grin and bank it.

There is a danger of being overexposed, but I've got my team around me looking out for that. That's another reason you've got to keep reinventing yourself, because people get bored of you. And when that happens, you've got to disappear for a bit or go off and do something different. I'm living on a crest of a wave at the minute, doing all these things and getting away with them. I feel lucky doing the TV and I'm pleased that most of it goes well and gives me and my family a nice life, which is the main thing. But it will come to an end, there will be a time when I get found out. I don't know when that's going to be, but I'll get the message that people have had enough of me and withdraw gracefully. I'll get over it, probably have a laugh about the fact I got away with it for so long. I've retired once from something I loved doing, so I'm not worried about retiring from something I never even dreamed of doing.

I turned 40 in 2017 and it didn't bother me. People keep saying to me, 'Are you having a mid-life crisis?' I'm not, but it still sounds weird when I tell people how old I am. I don't understand how it's happened. I look in the mirror sometimes and think, 'How have I got here? How have I already had a career?' It's strange to think that I'm halfway through my life and I've already done what I really wanted to do, which was to play cricket for Lancashire and England. I remember looking at my dad when he was 40 and thinking, 'Jesus, he's ancient.' That's weird, because I don't think I've lost my youth, and when I look in the mirror, I think I'll always look like I do.

I stand next to people my own age and feel like a child. I'll be milling about at the school gates and feel more like the kids than the parents. I like feeling like that. I'll get a reality check every now and again, when my head is willing and my body isn't. I'll go to the gym, my back will be killing me and I'll walk out stiff, as if I've got a piano on my back. My missus will ask if I'm all right and I'll sound like an old martyr – 'I'm fine! I'm fine!' – and I really am. There's no hiding from the fact my knees and ankles have gone, but I'll plough on regardless, won't give in. Maybe when I'm 50 things will be different, but you'll not find me sat in front of a fire with a rug over my legs any time soon.

I look at my daughter and think, 'How are you my kid? How did you get that big? You're more like my mate than a child.' But my kids are only just starting out on their lives, and I want them to have every opportunity to realise their ambitions. If that means me missing out on something, that's just the way it will have to be. I recently took my boys to the nets at Old Trafford and I loved those two hours more than any job I could do. I take them swimming, to the gym. I watch my daughter play netball, and afterwards I'll get a cuddle, some love and affection. Or we might just spend some time in the car together and have a nice chat. That small thing is better than anything I do for a living.

There's a quote I like: 'Some people are so poor, all they have is money.' Never a truer word was spoken. I've got what I need in terms of material wealth, which I am lucky and grateful for, and now I want to spend more time with my kids. When you're a professional sportsperson, there are lots of times when you put your family second. I didn't consider myself a selfish cricketer, but I was selfish about my career. When I took my cap or helmet off and saw the three lions, I might feel a pang of pride, and obviously it's great to represent your country at anything. But when I was batting or bowling, I never thought I was doing it for England. I never played cricket for my country, my family, the crowd or anyone else, I was doing it for myself. I scored runs because I liked scoring runs. And when I failed, I felt embarrassed, rather than feeling that I'd let anybody down.

I loved the feeling of winning and hated the feeling of losing. I'll watch the Olympics, see people standing on the podium with a silver medal around their neck and a big smile on their face and think, 'How can anyone lose and be happy?' I remember watching the diver Tom Daley winning bronze at the 2012 Olympics, and everyone was going mad and jumping in the pool. I couldn't understand it. I didn't see the Chinese lad who won the silver celebrating, he was probably in the shower crying. Sport is beautiful for so many reasons, but when you get to the highest level it's all about winning.

I don't understand people – sportspeople, businesspeople, whatever line of work they're in – entering into something and not wanting to be the best at it. I don't understand how a cricketer or a footballer can be happy being a squad player. Either it's not for you or you're not trying hard enough. In a way, I'm jealous of jobbing county cricketers – if they're happy with their lot, good luck to them. I just don't get how they can be. I had a go at boxing but quickly realised I was never going to be a world champion. So I wasn't going to waste any more time with it. I don't understand why people hang in there, doing things they're not going to be the best at.

When I was 11 years old, I was playing chess for Lancashire against Staffordshire, and they had this kid who wore a duffel coat and was the best player ever to walk the earth. I was basically put up against him as a sacrificial lamb, but he made this move and forgot to press his clock. The correct thing would have been to say, 'Mate, you've not pressed your clock.' But I knew I had no chance of beating him the conventional way, so I sat there, staring at the board and scratching my head. Forty minutes went by, the little flag on his clock dropped, and he started bellowing and crying. I got hauled up in front of the chess federation for unsportsmanlike behaviour, but when we left the place, I was high-fiving my teammates because we'd won. Nowadays I shy away from competition, because it brings out the worst in me.

Because cricket seemed so important, I sometimes took the simple pleasures for granted, or forgot about them completely. There were times, as terrible as it sounds, that playing for Lancashire and England became this blasé thing, and it should never be that way. I also got caught up in myself at times, especially after the 2005 Ashes. I got carried away, surrounded myself with the wrong people and became a bit narcissistic.

The family always gets a sportsperson at their worst. When you win, you're out celebrating with the lads. When you lose, you go home sulking. I sometimes didn't speak for three days after. I'd just sit there smouldering, playing the game over and over in my head. I've been guilty of doing that in my post-cricket career as well. I sometimes wonder if what made me a successful sportsperson has turned out to be my biggest weakness – the selfishness, that desire to score runs and take wickets, nothing ever being enough, always wanting more.

It was a nightmare for my wife at times. We had to move our wedding three times. I missed anniversaries, the birth of my second son. Rachael had to drive herself to hospital, give birth, drive herself home and then buy fish and chips for my mum and dad. She was very good about it, said that when my son is older, I can tell him I wasn't there because I was captaining England. Hopefully that will be good enough. When I found out, I was in the back of a car in Chandigarh, with Duncan Fletcher. Rachael phoned and I said, 'What's that in the background?'

'That's your son.'

'Oh, so you had the baby then?'

I said to Duncan, 'I've got a new baby boy.'

Duncan replied, 'Oh.'

Then there were the various misdemeanours which needed explaining. After the pedalo incident, I had to phone Rachael up, to warn her about the coming media storm.

'Hello, love.'

'Everything all right?'

'Yeah, just off to the press conference.'

'Think you'll win tomorrow?'

'I'm not playing. I've been banned.'

'What have you been banned for?'

'Are you sitting down?'

I then had to explain to my wife that her 27-year-old husband was spotted trying to get into a pedalo at 3 a.m in the middle of a World Cup.

There's a voraciousness in me. I'm like Pac-Man, chomping through life. In the sporting world, that works. In a family environment, it doesn't. Nothing is ever good enough and I'm always looking to the next thing before I've finished whatever it is I'm doing. But now, if I miss out on work and the money, because my family are calling the shots for once, I'm less bothered.

That's another reason I never could have become a pundit. I saw the other lads do it, spending all those months away from home, missing their kids growing up, and realised I had to take another route. But taking another route meant I was on less solid ground, taking jobs I wasn't exactly crazy about doing. Sometimes I'd be sat there in a far-flung hotel room thinking, 'What's all this for? When will it stop? I might only get another 40 summers, I might get less. And kids grow up so fast.'

I was doing something on the internet recently about who had the best beard, which meant I was missing one of the boy's cricket matches. Seriously, where would you rather be? Then again, other fathers go to work at 7:30 a.m., get home at 7:30 p.m., so they're probably missing out on more than me. I'm doing nothing different, I'm just weirder than most dads.

When I was in Australia filming a TV show, I was staying in a hotel in Sydney Harbour, which sounds wonderful, but didn't stop me having a wobble. I opened the curtains one morning and could see the Opera House, the Harbour Bridge, the sea, the sun, and all these people out and about enjoying themselves. But I was on my own. There might be people reading this and thinking, 'He's in Sydney, he's on the telly – what's his problem? He doesn't know how lucky he is.' But it doesn't matter where you are or how nice your hotel is, if you're missing the people you love, it can be horrible.

That's not to say I'd ever quit working completely. As much as I love being at home and around the family, I couldn't just do nothing. I need to be stimulated, mentally and physically. What would I do all day? Sit about and watch TV? Go to the gym, come home and do what? Have a cup of tea and twiddle my thumbs? Play golf on the same course every day? I'd end up topping myself.

CHAPTER 21

PARENTS

Doing things my way

I'm proud as punch of all three of my kids. If one of my kids does something amazing, something they've worked really hard to achieve, I get more out of that than anything I've ever done or ever will. I am proud of things I achieved during my cricket career, but watching your kids do their thing is on another level entirely.

I never thought I'd want my boys to play cricket, not so much because of the game, but because of the pressure. But they love it. Watching my boys on the field wearing the Lancashire rose just like I did when I was a kid makes me incredibly proud. But I get so nervous watching them, more so than when I played. I could control my performances to an extent, but I've got no control over them. I just want them to do well, because it makes or breaks their day. Cricket is a strange sport, in that you make one mistake and you're off. In football, you can make a terrible pass or score an own goal and still have 90 minutes to make up for it.

My daughter is a good athlete but singing is more her thing. She sings solos at school. My nan, who died a few years ago, used to sing 'Somewhere Over the Rainbow' with me when I was a kid, and my daughter sang it in front of the whole school. That brought a tear to the eyes.

Commitment is a big thing for me. I always say to my kids, whatever it is you do, do it the best you can. In sport, I want them to be ruthless. When they're practising their batting, and I'm feeding the ball into the bowling machine, I don't want them to be thinking about anything else apart from what they're doing. I have fun with them and I can handle them failing, but I can't handle them not trying. And because I've seen both sides of it, they can't get one over on me, I know if they're giving it their all or not.

After the boys have played, we'll go and have a chat about things, discuss whether they've done what they're capable of. They're at the age where I've started to be a bit more blunt with them. If I'm hard, it's only because I want them to strive to be better. I can accept failure, but I cannot get my head around anyone not trying. I get annoyed, and that stems from the fact I wasted the first part of my career. They were years I never got back, and I don't want my kids to ever have any feelings of regret. There have been times when I've been in the nets with one of my boys and I've both got frustrated and said things I shouldn't have. But I want them to make it for themselves, not for me. I also want them to do something they love and are passionate about. For me, it was cricket. For them, it might be something else.

I can see the passion they have for the game, but it's different. I wasn't from a privileged background, financially at least. In terms of love and support, I couldn't fault it. My mum and dad took us everywhere, slept in the car when I was a kid on tours, broke the bank for my kit. From that comes a desire to pay them back. But I also had to do it myself to some degree. Now, sport is very different. Academies are fantastic in some respects, because of the level of teaching and the opportunities they provide. But I do think they can affect a young player's hunger. A lot is done for them – a lot of the nitty-gritty that used to shape players – so that when they're challenged in the real world, it's more difficult to work things out.

I don't think it's a coincidence that some of the best foot-ballers come from poorer backgrounds, so for me it's about finding the balance between giving the kids what they need and not spoiling them. When I take the boys to Old Trafford nets, they're rubbing shoulders with Lancashire players. Imagine that? That's normal for them and it's great, but it's a completely different world from the one I grew up in, and that worries me a little bit. It might be a better way of doing things, it's just not the way I'm used to.

I loved playing against the posh kids, with all the latest gear, that's where I got some of my hunger. I was offered scholarships to schools from all over the country, but I didn't go, because the men's cricket I was playing was a better grounding than schoolboy cricket. I was tempted to send my kids to state schools. Instead, for various reasons, they go to private schools, get a great education and, bless them, they appreciate that. But I also don't want them to take anything for granted. I sit on the boundary watching my boys play at this wonderful school with playing fields as far as the eye can see, and think, 'Wow, this is incredible.' They do play on more basic club grounds for the county, so maybe their cricket education is actually more balanced than mine was. But I sometimes I wish they were playing on grounds with dog shit all over them and smackheads in the playground next door.

When I played cricket as a kid, my dad was in the same team, so if anyone had a go at me, he'd step in. If anyone had a go at one of my sons, I'd do the same. In some ways I'm a pushy parent, but I'm not one of those idiots who shouts at them from the boundary, telling them what shot they should have played or where to move the field. I think those kinds of parents should be shot.

I watch the boys play football as well, but the only time I've ever shouted anything was when one of them had their shirt hanging out. I have to stand behind a rope, which I thought was weird at first, because I'm a 40-year-old man, not a teenage nutcase. But when you see how some of the other parents behave you realise why the railing is there. There will be some 15-year-old kid refereeing and he's being shouted at by grown men. Grown men. Shouting. At a 15-year-old referee. There will be 20-stone blokes, who were probably bloody useless footballers anyway, screaming at their kids, 'Get here! Go there! Get rid of it!' I'll be standing there thinking, 'What the hell are you doing?'

I was watching one of my lads bat a few years ago and this dad kept appealing against him from the boundary. I walked up to him, tapped him on the shoulder and said, 'Mate, get a life. Think about it for a second – you're appealing against an eight-year-old boy. What are you doing?' I genuinely love watching my boys play, but I struggle sitting on the boundary with other parents, because I just can't deal with the chat. I might not know about a lot of things, but cricket is one of them. I'll be sat there listening to mums and dads going on about what happened in the last game, what people scored, what so and so did wrong, what so and so should improve on, and it drives me nuts. I try to sit with my mate Nigel, just to be away from it, because it can seriously ruin my day.

That's the worst thing about kids – parents. You know when the kids are in the pool on holiday? You see them throwing a ball about with some other kids and then they start chatting? When that happens, that's when you've got to be on your guard. The last thing you want is your kids bringing over their new mates, because that means one of their parents will soon come wandering over, saying stuff like, 'Oh, we're taking the kids to the waterpark this afternoon, would your kids like to come?'

No!

'Oh, we're having lunch in this lovely restaurant today, would you and your wife like to come?'

No!

'Oh, we're thinking of having drinks in the bar after dinner, would you like to join us?'

I don't drink!

I recommend very dark glasses, because eye contact is a killer. And when I get trapped with strange, annoying parents, things can get very ugly.

CHAPTER 22

FUN WHILE IT LASTED

Dealing with brickbats

One of the problems with sport is that everyone thinks they know best. You'll have a football manager getting paid God knows how much money but the lad sitting in Wetherspoons on his 15th Guinness or the bloke driving a white van knows better. They honestly think they could manage Manchester United. What is wrong with these people? The lack of awareness beggars belief.

I'd be batting, make a mistake, and people would jump all over me. I'd think, 'Do you not think we practise? Do you really think I wanted to do that?' One game against the West Indies at Lord's, I went out to bat last over before lunch and Omari Banks, a spinner, was bowling. He was dreadful, but swanned around as if he owned the place, so I always wanted to smash him. He lobbed his first ball up and I launched him straight over his head for six. Before he'd even bowled the next ball I thought, 'Whatever it is, I'll just pat it back and play for lunch.' He lobbed it up, same as the first ball, I should have launched him again, tried to block it instead, got in a muddle and was bowled.

As I was walking up the steps of the pavilion, someone hit me over the head with a rolled-up newspaper and I heard this really posh voice behind me: 'Fun while it lasted, Flintoff!' I turned round with my fist cocked, ready to drop someone, and saw this little old man scuttling off through the door. In the end, I'd walk through the Long Room at Lord's, on my way out to bat, letting big belches out, just to upset the old members in their MCC blazers and ties.

In India, I was on the back of the bus on the way back from a match, after we'd been beaten again, desperate for a wee. Someone said, 'Just piss out the back', so I slid the window open, was doing a big wee and a tour coach went past, full of supporters. Not a Barmy Army tour coach, but a serious one, full of rich middle-class people staying in the finest hotels. When I arrived at the airport, all these supporters were coming up to me and telling me what a disgrace I was – not for weeing out the back of the bus, but for the shot I played to get out. I was thinking, 'Hang on a minute, I was just weeing out the back of a bus, and you're lecturing me about the shot I played? Weird'.

If you're buying a ticket or you have a Sky subscription, of course you've got the right to criticise. When I pay to watch a film, I'll have an opinion about it, and I can say what I want. But I struggle when I hear people talking about things they know very little about. I'll listen to people talking about the technicalities of cricket, when they've never played at anywhere near the highest level, and I'll be bemused. More than anything else, I find it funny. I hate it when people say, 'They didn't want it enough', or, 'They wanted it more than them.' Or they'll speculate on a player's state of mind when they have absolutely no idea what's going on in that person's head.

If you play a shocking shot or you're visibly fat or are hanging out of your arse, fine. But criticism of a player's skills and techniques wouldn't happen in any other business. Imagine if they made surgery a spectator sport and people crowded into an operating theatre to watch a kidney transplant. They wouldn't all sit there going, 'Oh no, I wouldn't have done that, that's all wrong. I would have removed that bit first...' But in sport, everyone has an opinion, whether they've played that sport or not. It's the strangest thing.

I received untold stick after the Ashes Down Under in 2006–07, but everything was against us on that tour, from the very beginning. There was a team unveiling at the Oval, and I was selected with the rest of the team as captain, which meant I didn't get to pick my squad. I was looking around at the lads and thinking, 'I'm not sure I would have picked four or five of you.' I didn't get on with the coach, Duncan Fletcher. My best player, Marcus Trescothick, went home ill. Harmy's head wasn't right either, and I was injured and had no form.

I'd do it again, simply because you can't turn it down – on my CV, it says I was England captain – but, looked at another way, I was mad to accept it and should have trusted my instincts. Andrew Strauss had been doing a decent interim job and I knew deep down that my best role in the team was leading by performance and being a right-hand man to the captain.

When it all went to shit and the Aussies were hammering us, I had to carry the can for it. I behaved inappropriately at times, and drank a bit too much, but they were symptoms of what was going on in the background. I'm quite happy to admit I wasn't suited to the job, but it wasn't just me to blame.

I often say I was a terrible England skipper, but for a while I was quite good. In fact, I've had so many people tell me what a bad England captain I was, I'm now going to blow my own trumpet and say I was brilliant. We drew a series in India, hammered them in Mumbai, the first time we'd beaten them there in God knows how long, and I was named player of the series. At the time, everyone was going on about how the responsibility of captaincy had brought the best out in me. I was tactically average, but I led a young team from the front and everyone bought into it. I gave one team-talk naked, before singing Johnny Cash's 'Ring of Fire' and bowling India out. If you can't be inspired by that, you're in the wrong game! We then drew with Sri Lanka, and it was during that series that I got injured. Everything went downhill from there.

We played like a team of herberts on that Ashes tour, and the biggest herbert was leading them. I can take bad performances, that just happens. People play poorly and there's not much you can do about it. But after we lost in Perth, which meant we'd lost the Ashes after just three Tests, there was a chat in the dressing room over a few beers, and players were saying they could have done more to prepare for going on tour. I was thinking, 'Hang on a minute, I've done everything I can to make the tour, we've been hammered, and now you're telling me you could have done more?' I'm not denying I got things wrong on that tour, I was far from blameless, but I had to carry the can for everyone. That annoyed me, and I can't forgive some of those players for that.

I tell you what is absolute bollocks, the notion of team spirit. The media are always going on about it, but it rarely exists. When everything is great, players are performing well and the team are winning, then people start claiming it's all down to team spirit. But it's got nothing to do with team spirit, it just means everyone is happy because everything is great, players are performing well and the team are winning. And it's the same if you're getting beaten – it's got nothing to do with team spirit, it just means everyone has got the hump because you're getting dicked on. The closest thing to team spirit I experienced was with Lancashire after my comeback from injury. I thought we had team spirit in 2005, but it soon evaporated when the team was tested and things started going wrong on the tour of Pakistan. In hindsight, that team that regained the Ashes in 2005 was just a bloody good team playing well.

Once you start losing in Australia, that's when you need some of that mysterious team spirit most. But when the shit hit the fan on that tour, that's when the back-stabbing started, people started forming their own little splinter groups and looking after number one. I couldn't be doing with that. That was exactly when the coach and the players needed to show their togetherness, muck in and take it on the chin together. Instead, people preferred to cover their own backs, hanging one or two people out to dry.

Poor old Harmy got hammered for bowling that first ball of the series, the one that was so wide I took it at second slip. Ashley Giles got hammered for dropping Ricky Ponting on the boundary. I got hammered for being a bit shit. I could have done more. But I couldn't help looking round the dressing room and thinking, 'Oh, right, it's like that is it? You scored a few runs or took a couple of wickets and you're not worried about anybody else. Well done.' Actually, the few players who were in form should have been helping those who weren't.

I suppose the Aussies saw that series as payback for 2005, but it wasn't even a contest because we weren't in any kind of condition to take them on. In the first game, we got beaten by the Prime Minister's XI by 160-odd runs in a one-day match, so forget about Ponting, Warne, McGrath and the rest. The worst part is, cricket is not like football, where it only goes on for 90 minutes, and even if you're 3–0 down you've still got an outside chance. With cricket, you usually know from miles out that you're going to lose, so by the time you finally get beaten, you're already feeling numb. That tour was 25 days of feeling crushed. Actually, probably about 18 days, because most Tests ended early.

When the final Test was over, I had to give a speech after the presentation ceremony. We'd just had our pants pulled down, been hammered 5–0, what was I supposed to say? I obviously thanked everyone, but I don't know what I was thanking them for. I wanted to point at my team and say, 'You lot, useless', before pointing to the Aussies and saying, 'You lot, great. Now

I'm going home…' But before I could go home, I had to deal with the England supporters, people shouting things like 'You were a disgrace' or 'We saved up all our lives for this!' What did they want me to do? I felt bad, but I also felt powerless. Part of me felt like saying, 'Look, sorry, but you're in Australia, it's a wonderful place, just take a holiday and enjoy the beaches.'

It's hard for people to understand, but something like that can take a huge personal toll on a sportsperson. I'd lost any sense of perspective, convinced myself that the defeat would define me as a person, that it was the only thing that mattered. I struggled to look people in the eye after that series, didn't want to be around anyone. Me and my missus went to America, where we were staying in a lovely reserve on a golf course, and I said to her, 'Tell you what, why don't we just cash in and open a cafe?' I actually started looking at houses in brochures. But as soon as I started training again, I thought, 'Not a chance. If they're all back at home saying I'm finished, I have to prove them wrong.'

CHAPTER 23

NOT BY A LONG CHALK

What happens next?

I don't understand bucket lists. People say, 'I want to get to 40 and do this', but why wait until you're 40? Just go and do it. My bucket list consisted of playing cricket for Lancashire and England; everything else has been a bonus.

If I'm being brutally honest, I still feel like a part of me is missing. I've done some incredible things since I retired, but I still desperately want to be a cricketer, walking down the steps at Lord's with that feeling in my tummy, so nervous because it means so much. Nothing will ever replace that feeling. But I'm lucky. A lot of people retire from cricket and don't know what to do with their lives. When they perhaps should have been preparing for a post-cricket career, they were too busy drinking shots of Tabasco in the dressing room.

One day they were enjoying a life they thought would never end, the next day it had all stopped. More should have been done to help, people should have been employed to explain all the wonderful things that were out there beyond cricket.

I spend a lot of time thinking about how weird my life is. I'll be lying in bed, staring at the ceiling, and my mind will be like Moss Side on a Saturday night – you wouldn't want to go there on your own. My mind can go anywhere, to wondering if we're living in a matrix, to whether aliens exist or if we've got milk in the fridge. I might be coming up with a new job idea or whacky business venture. I'm not really in control of it, so I just run with it.

I also ask myself, 'What's the point?' all the time. We're here for such a short space of time, but why are we here? How do I make the most of my time on earth? Am I meant to do something special? Surely everyone has a purpose? What is it? I can't have been put here to hit and throw a ball about? Or maybe I was?

I look back at my cricket career and think, 'What was that all about?' When you're playing, scoring a few runs against India or trying to get Wasim Jaffer out seems like the most important thing in the world. I'd get out for a duck and it would be like my world was caving in. But I just missed a ball. That's fine. And let's be honest, not many people are that bothered about cricket anyway. And why should they be? Most of the time, cricket is a load of blokes standing around in a field. While you're playing professional sport, you get trapped inside this little, all-consuming bubble, but after you've packed it in, you have a chuckle and think, 'What a knob.'

Even before I retired, having kids changed my outlook. All of a sudden, cricket was no longer the most important thing in my life. If I had a bad day, although I'd still beat myself up about it, I knew that my family still loved me, I'd get a cuddle off the kids when I got home and the sun would come up tomorrow. Now I'm working in the entertainment industry, I am very aware of its triviality. Musical theatre – it's brilliant, and I love it, but how is it even a thing? You pay 100 quid to watch adults dress up and play for a couple of hours. And I've ended up doing it.

It's not like I'm some pop star who suddenly turns around and says, 'I want to be taken seriously!' But I can understand the sentiment. When I'm dressed as a woman in New York about to perform drag, or speedskating in Streatham, or standing in the street with a cardboard cut-out of a man called Lewis, I do find myself thinking, 'Why? What? How?' It's a job, and it's all good fun, but I'd like to do stuff that's a bit more worthy, a bit more meaningful, something I'm really proud of and really means something to people. It's about finding something that is worthy of your time, something that is going to satisfy you.

Comedy would be the obvious route, given my stint on *A League of Their Own* and some of the other stuff I've done so far. I did a Sky Comedy Short a couple of years back called *Pacino & Bert.* I play this shy bloke walking his dog on the beach in Southport. One day, I pass this girl, who I like the look of. After a few days, I pluck up the courage to speak to her, but I keep messing it up. Finally, I resolve to ask her out, put my best gear on, and just as I'm approaching her, this beach patrol bloke – played by Mick Johnson from *Brookside* – comes running over and tells us we can't walk our dogs on the beach during summer. We both get sent on our separate ways and never see her again. It was quite tragic. A fella called Dan Maier wrote it, and it's about missed opportunities and regrets, a subject very close to my heart.

I've started writing a couple of sitcoms, one about a gym and another about cycling. They're both about my experiences, the characters that pop up from day to day, and the challenge is trying to write exaggerated versions of them. I'd love to write something and for people to say, 'Wow, that's brilliant, how's he done that?' I'd also like to do stand-up. I did some dates a few years ago, but it was more telling stories than stand-up. So next time I'd like to do it properly, a 30- or 40-date tour. I've started writing stuff about sex, trying to get a girlfriend when I was a kid, mental illness, and I'd like to do some sets at some smaller comedy clubs and build it from there. I know some people in the game – Jack Whitehall, Jimmy Carr, Micky Flanagan – and while I don't want them to swing gigs for me, they can give me some guidance.

Sometimes you're a bit reticent to speak to comedians about it, in case they think it's ridiculous, but when I mentioned it to Lee Mack, he just said, 'Why not? Have a go.' A man after my own heart. You often hear people say that doing stand-up must be the most terrifying thing in the world. But walking out onstage at the Apollo Theatre means nothing compared to walking out to bat at Lord's. So why not swing the bat and see what happens?

Straight acting is something I'm talking about doing at the moment. I've been to some castings, there's some stuff going on with Kay Mellor, one of whose dramas I've already appeared in, and I've also had talks with Lynda La Plante. She sent me a script about a dog, which was actually quite dark. Let's just say it had a bit more gravitas than talking to puppets with Gary Lineker, which is one of the gigs I've had.

I don't want a walk-on part on *Corrie*, or a two-minute spot in a drama. If I'm going to act, I want to do it fully. I sometimes think my ambition outweighs my talent, but then I tell myself I just need to graft and learn the craft, just as I did with cricket. I'd like to play a lead role, and something dark, gritty and meaty, like a baddie in one of those Scandinavian-style dramas. But while I would like to act, if I don't, I'll be all right, because it's all a bonus anyway. Would I say no if Hollywood came knocking? It's a long shot, but who knows what might happen. And if Jack Whitehall can carve out a career over there, there might just be hope for me and Jamie Redknapp.

I'm also involved in property. Manchester is the obvious place to build because it's booming, but I wanted to build stuff in Preston because it's my home town and there are more challenges in the smaller Lancashire towns and cities. I played for Lancashire, want to see my region thriving, but a lot of those old industrial towns are in need of regeneration. The town centres are desolate, and you need things in the centre of towns for people to visit. It would have been gratifying to drive through Preston and think, 'We built that.' It's not like I want a pat on the back or anything, or plan to run bus tours or put a big sign on it saying, 'Fred Flintoff built this.' I want to play a role in improving places that are dear to me, making them better for everyone.

I've spent a lot of time in Manchester over the past couple of years and the homelessness is terrible. My youngest is horrified by it – 'Dad, why are all these people on the street?' It's not one or two, it's hundreds. I was at a property conference and everyone was showing videos of these massive skyscrapers, 50 storeys high, worth hundreds of millions of pounds, but part of me was thinking, 'We're trying to build these things up, but look what's happening on the ground.'

I buy food and take it round to give to homeless people, but that's not even scratching the surface. We'd like to get involved with the mayor, Andy Burnham, because what's the point in having all these shiny buildings for people to live in and when they walk out the front door there are homeless people everywhere, unable to clothe or feed themselves? We hear all these speeches from people saying we need to improve our cities, and Burnham is having a crack, but that should start on the ground, literally.

Prevention is often better than cure, and it's about understanding why these people become homeless in the first place. People who are homeless don't just need a house, they need emotional and practical help. They need someone to give them a chance, someone to reach down and help them back to their feet. Like any social care, preventative care is expensive. As with mental illness or addiction, which often go hand in hand with homelessness, the initial outlay for preventative care might seem huge, but in the long run it will be far cheaper than spending hundreds of millions on temporary shelter.

I've had issues with mental illness and addiction, so I know how it feels when you can see no way out. Social inequality and injustice make me angry, and you've got to challenge things at the root rather than wait until it's overgrown and out of control. It's another thing that makes me wonder whether the world is real. This isn't the slums of India, this is right outside people's front doors in Manchester. It's everywhere, and it makes me pinch myself.

We had our own charity until a few years back, and now we raise money for others. Famous or wealthy people should give back, otherwise you're just taking all the time. It's not just the free bikes and clothes, it's also that as a celebrity, you expect everyone to buy into whatever it is you're doing, whether it's a gameshow a musical or something you're trying to flog. I'll be doing an advert for a shaver, thinking, 'Is this shaver such a good deal that I'm helping anyone's life?' It's not that I'm embarrassed about trying to flog a shaver, it's just that trying to flog anything seems so futile at times. I think anyone in a privileged position should see the bigger picture and contribute to society.

I'm not a communist, I don't think everything should be shared out equally because you get lazy people who will take advantage of that. But people who are less fortunate than others should be looked after properly. There's no sense in the world. How is it that someone who saves people's lives in A&E doesn't get paid as much as someone who kicks a ball about for a living? I understand the economics, but it's still absurd. How is it that the NHS is struggling? The very fact it's struggling tells you that there has to be a more sensible way of dividing up the money and that we don't have our priorities right. Do we really need more submarines?

Politics is something I might like to have a go at, mainly because the people doing it at the moment don't seem to be doing a very good job. It's easy to have a pop at politicians, but at least they're having a go. At the same time, I see our politicians on the telly and think, 'Really? Is that the best we've got?' And I can see myself shouting on the Commons backbenches, making all those noises and having a bit of a crack when someone else is trying to speak. I don't understand how anything gets done, it's one of the most ridiculous things I've ever seen. If one person says they're going to do something, another person will say they're going to do something else. Everybody realises the right thing needs to be done, but they all have to have a row about it instead. You never hear somebody in the House of Commons say, 'Actually, that's a fair point'. Or, 'I disagree, but maybe we can have a nice chat about it and reach a compromise'. Instead, they're all heckling each other. That can't possibly be the best way of going about things.

We've got all these parties arguing about this, that and the other, but why don't we just get the best people from whatever party together and try to sort everything out? If you were running a company, you'd do everything you could to hire the best people so as to run that company in the best possible way. But politics doesn't work like that. I know different parties have different ideologies, but in times of great crisis – which is what we seem to be in – there has to be a better way than just arguing all the time.

While I say I might like to have a go at politics, I'm not 100 per cent sure what Brexit is. Is anyone? I know we're leaving. Or are we? I've been watching *Newsnight*, all these other political programmes, and I'm still none the wiser. It always seems to be two people from opposing parties arguing with each other, and I'm not even sure they know what they're arguing about. A lot of it seems to be point-scoring, adults behaving like children.

I question people's motives. Nigel Farage was just having a laugh. He went on and on about wanting to leave Europe and once we voted for it, he legged it. And now he's back again, driving around in his bus, with 'Leave Means Leave' written all over it. When we are actually out, I assume he'll be telling everyone we didn't do it properly. You see Farage on TV and he's a slippery fella, very tricky to pin down. They chuck it all at him and he's got an answer for everything. He appeals to people who think eating pizza is a bit suspect. They don't like what's going on with the country, are fed up with the status quo and think England should go it alone. But I'm not sure we can. It's similar to Donald Trump and all this stuff about making America great again and putting America first. People whinge about Trump, but you can see how he got in. He had a go, was different to the traditional choices and is now trying to do what he said he was going to do. It makes me wonder if, one day, we'll have someone from *Love Island* running our country.

I love Preston, I love Lancashire and I'm a proud Englishman. That's probably where it stops – I don't have the same pride about being British, and I also don't see myself as European, which isn't the same as saying I'm a Brexiteer. Maybe it's because I played for England and that's all I ever wanted to do. Saying that, I don't really know what it is to be English. All I know is that of all the places I've been in the world, I love England more than any of them. I go to the Lake District, the Yorkshire Dales or the New Forest and think, 'Why would you want to be anywhere else?' I like what I know and I get fed up with people putting England down. It's got things wrong with it, but where hasn't?

But some of the stuff that makes people feel like proud Englishmen just seems slightly iffy to me. I see a Union Jack or George Cross hanging from someone's house and automatically think they're a right-wing wrong 'un. I grew up in a multi-cultural society in Preston, playing cricket I was surrounded by West Indians and Asians, and that enriched my childhood and continues to enrich me as an adult. It's to England's gain that we've got all these people from different parts of the world. Someone might see a person of colour in Manchester and assume they're Indian or Pakistani, but that person might have a better idea of Englishness than the person making the assumption, because they've seen and experienced more of the country and more of the world.

We chose Brexit, that's what we wanted. We can't have another referendum. Although some people are now saying we can. It's so confusing. What happens if Brexit wins again? Do we make it best of five? Ultimately, if we're in or out, we need to get on with it. I know Brexit might have terrible consequences, but I have to see the funny side of it, otherwise my head would explode. I was watching *Newsnight* recently, and the head of the sandwich corporation was on there, saying that Brexit would be terrible for the sandwich industry because the ingredients would be unavailable or too expensive. Avocadoes were mentioned, certain lettuces. I was thinking, 'If this is the sum of it, we'll be all right. They might have to stockpile avocadoes in Chiswick, but we'll get over it.'

CHAPTER 24

WHO DECIDES WHAT MATTERS?

Going back to basics

I was driving through Manchester the other day, looking at people making their way to work, and I couldn't help noticing how miserable everyone seemed. It was like one of those old pictures by Lowry, everyone was rushing around, bent over, with their heads down. It made me realise that not much has changed since he painted those pictures almost 100 years ago, except now it's shops and call centres instead of mills.

There was this one fella – I can picture him now, big man, bald, in his forties, wearing a shirt and tie – who appeared from under the railway bridge and looked so flustered and unhappy. It bothered me. He was probably rushing to a meeting to talk about the targets he's not hitting. I looked at him and thought, 'Mate, what's the point? It doesn't matter if you're five minutes late for your meeting. Nobody's going to care. And if they do, bollocks to them.' People get hung up on the wrong things. We don't know how it all started, if the world is going to end tomorrow and what's going to happen when we all die, and this fella is busting a gut to get to his office, where he'll spend the next eight hours staring at a computer screen.

Who decides what matters? One day it's Brexit, which is an end-of-days scenario, even though no one really knows what it is, the next it's Adil Rashid being picked for England. If people stopped caring about everything, the world would be a far better place. I'm quite laid-back about most things, until I see people not being laid-back about things I think they should be laid-back about. There are so many things in the world that matter, but we spend our time worrying about things that absolutely don't matter. Geoffrey Boycott comes straight out of a quadruple open heart bypass surgery and starts having a go at Adil Rashid. Come on, Geoffrey. Get a life, mate.

It's bizarre what people worry about, what makes us happy and makes us sad. I remember when I was watching the 2012 Olympics. One of our canoeists won a gold medal and when the anthem came on, I started welling up. I had to get a grip of myself, physically get up and say, 'What are you doing? He's a canoeist in a false lake in Eton Dorney. It's meaningless.'

I've never been much of a cryer. I cried in India when I couldn't score a run and got out to one of the worst bowlers ever, which was the final straw. I had a tear in my eye at the end of my last Test, because I felt a bit robbed and was standing there thinking, 'I'm fitter and bowling better than I've ever done, but I'm never going to do this again.' But I certainly didn't cry when we regained the Ashes, I just got on the pop with the lads. I had a tear in my eye when my lad scored his first hundred, but it was never going to escalate to full-blown blubbing. It's not like I try not to cry, and it's not like I've got a problem with men crying, it's just not something that comes naturally.

Why is Mo Farah running 5,000m and 10,000m even a thing? Who decided it was a thing in the first place? Why am I bothered? I was cheering along with everyone else when he won all his races, because I was proud of what he was doing. But it makes no sense. Why does anyone care that someone can throw a javelin further than everyone else? It's just people throwing sticks. Triple-jump, what's that all about? Why does anyone in their right mind care that someone is brilliant at hop, skip and jumping into a sand pit? Greg Rutherford jumped a bit further than everyone else at the 2012 Olympics and people were calling for him to be knighted. He jumps for a living! How is that helping anyone? Does it matter if he's helping anyone?

Big things don't really bother me, but a door or cupboard slamming will. Or a football bouncing on a path. Punch me in the face and I'll be fine. The other day, there were no blue socks in the drawer. There were white socks, black socks, but I wanted blue socks. I said to my missus, 'Have you got any blue socks?' She didn't hear me, but I was running a bit late, flapping, and we ended up having a row about it.

When I got home, she tried to make me apologise. I pulled out the line, 'I don't ask for much. I just wanted some blue socks...' I don't like myself for it – who gets bothered by not having any blue socks, but isn't bothered by Brexit, which could adversely affect my kids' lives? Especially when I've just been going on about people being bothered about things they shouldn't be bothered about. I was breaking my own rule, which bothered me... Fact is, there's no real middle ground with me, either I'm horizontal or going mad about something trivial, like not being able to find some blue socks.

I don't really see myself as a non-conformist, I just conform to what I believe is the right way of living. If I agree with something I'm told, that's fine. If I don't, I'm not going to pretend I do. If I feel I need to do something to improve, I'll commit to it fully. If not, I won't. When we used to do the beep test in training, I'd say to the coach, 'What score do I need to get? Twelve? OK, I'll get 12 then.' And I'd get 12 and stop. Just give me a bat and ball.

Why would anyone do something they disagree with? It baffles me. It's one of the reasons my head is so messed up. So many people spend a large chunk of their lives doing something they don't enjoy. They're no different from bees, or those ants you see carrying leaves on their backs, it's just on a bigger scale. They're all just working to keep things working, but to what end?

People work all their life to get to 60 or 65 and then when they retire, they don't do owt. Surely that's the wrong way around? You go to school and you'd sooner be doing something else, you spend your best adult years working when you'd sooner be doing something else, and then you retire, put a rug on your legs, eat an ice cream and stare out to sea.

Just knock everything down and build mud huts, then we can go back to living off the land. Then again, imagine if you had seven billion people all out hunting and gathering, all the animals would be gone in about an hour, Ricky Gervais would start kicking off on Twitter and we'd soon be eating each other.

I'll be honest, I don't know what the future holds. The fun is in not knowing. And by then, the world might have ended anyway. Or we might have been abducted by aliens. Or I might be a cockroach. Whatever it is I do, wherever and whatever I am, as long as I still have my family and close friends around me, I'll be all right. What's more important than that?